OPEN House!

An Insider's Tour of the Secret World

of Residential Real Estate for

Agents, Sellers, and Buyers

JOEY SHEEHAN

M000312100

Copyright © 2021 by Joey Sheehan

All rights reserved. No part of this publication in print or in electronic format may be reproduced, stored in a retrieval system, or transmitted in any form or by any means, electronic, mechanical, photocopying, recording, or otherwise without the prior written permission of the publisher.

The scanning, uploading, and distribution of this book without permission is a theft of the author's intellectual property. If you would like permission to use material from the book (other than for review purposes), please contact joey.sheehan@foxroach.com. Thank you for your support of the author's rights.

Published by Canterbury Books

ISBN: 978-1-64704-327-8 (eBook)
ISBN: 978-1-64704-328-5 (Paperback)
ISBN: 978-1-64704-329-2 (Dust-jacket)

FOR AL.

CONTENTS

PART ONE
DRAMATIS PERSONAE
(AGENT, SELLER, BUYER)

PART TWO
THE IMPLICATIONS OF WORKING AT RISK
(AGENT)

PART THREE
MAXIMIZING YOUR LISTING EXPERIENCE
(SELLER)

PART FOUR
BEING ON TOP OF YOUR HOME PURCHASE
(BUYER)

PART FIVE
APPROACHING SAFE HARBOR

A BRIEF DISCLAIMER

To make this guide to residential real estate as broadly appealing as possible, I have set the scene in a nameless American suburb. It is an affluent area whose real estate trends, by and large, mirror those of the rest of the country. As a Realtor, I have been affiliated with a single brokerage company that shall also remain nameless. It is much larger today than when I first joined.

Sprinkled throughout *OPEN HOUSE!* are numerous illustrative stories culled from my long career in the real estate industry. Their purpose is to help drive home (no pun intended) principles and practices that an agent, seller, or buyer should either embrace or avoid at all costs in any contemplated real estate transaction. Names of clients, the location of their properties, and other identifying information have been altered to protect the privacy of those concerned. The identities of fellow Realtors appearing in the book have been disguised as well.

A NOTE ON PRONOUN USAGE

Before Harvard University Press published my first book, a copy editor had disapprovingly noted my "sexist" use of pronouns. By virtue of writing a biography of a renowned traditional Chinese scholar of the late imperial / early Republican period, a work featuring not a single female, I apparently was guilty of a superfluity of "he's," a vacuity of "she's," and an insufficient number of gender-neutral pronouns to correct the imbalance. That painful experience made me sensitive about what procedure to follow in this book.

Arbitrarily—for simplicity's sake—I have chosen to use the pronoun "she" for all unnamed agents even though my profession has a respectable number of male practitioners. Meanwhile, to balance things out, you will see that I use the pronoun "he" to refer to any unnamed seller or buyer. I hope this literary "shorthand" will meet with my readers' approval.

PROLOGUE

My husband believes home sellers are nuts. He also believes home buyers are nuts. As for the real estate agents who make careers out of servicing these folks, he pretty much regards us as nutty too ("damn crazy" were his exact words). I won't protest Al.'s harsh assessment of all concerned. Via this particular Realtor, he's been exposed over the years to so many real estate-related contretemps, legal snafus, financing tangles, structural issues, environmental problems, and bizarre emergencies of all kinds (at all hours) that I'm actually relieved he considers my industry "damn crazy" and lets it go at that.

In truth, residential real estate *is* a business like no other. It's not rational like other businesses because the commodity being bought or sold is a home rather than a car or a refrigerator, and everybody knows that a man's home is his castle. People get touchy about their castles—you can trust me on this—in a way they don't about anything else, including even their children and their investment portfolios. That's just the way things are.

I have been working in this unique, intermittently explosive professional environment for over three decades now. With that much experience under my belt, I am in a perfect position to pull back the curtain on a veiled industry whose nonetheless essential services are used by two-thirds of Americans during their adult lives. You may, of course, imagine that you already know roughly what a Realtor does, but I suspect you've seen only the tip of the iceberg. A professional real estate agent has *lots* of depth, just like an iceberg.

Another analogy is a duck. A duck progresses calmly across the pond (that's what observers see), but below the surface the duck is paddling like the devil. To her clientele, a successful Realtor makes selling or buying a residence seem effortless. Behind the scenes, however, she strives tirelessly to keep her transactions smoothly on course despite the glitches, setbacks, and occasional catastrophes that inevitably arise. Are you curious about what all that furious metaphorical paddling is accomplishing for the 66 percent? Good! I will tell you.

Books on real estate tend to fall into several categories. One category concerns *investing* in it, which accounts for an enormous number of works but is irrelevant for present purposes. The focus of a second popular category is enhancing the productivity of real estate agents for the purpose of increasing their sales volume and hence their earnings, preferably substantially. A third category of books on real estate, closely related to the second one, focuses on a salesman's personal motivation. Ostensibly its aim is to develop the Realtor's all-important attitude, but the goal of this cultivation is principally to instill a superior mindset that will increase that agent's productivity. These connected categories make sense from a real estate agent's point of view—if we don't make sales, we don't eat—but are of no interest to the actual home-selling and home-buying public.

Besides works on how to make a fortune by either investing in real estate or selling real estate services, there is a fourth category of real estate books, or at least there should be. This one concerns the lived experience of the 66 percent of American adults that sell or buy homes as well as the Realtors who facilitate their doing so. As a work in this putative genre, my insider's exposure of the inner workings of America's residential real estate industry aims to both entertain and enlighten. It is a bit of magic, really, when a seller's agent, a seller, a buyer's agent, and a buyer can all work collaboratively enough together that in due course a nice fat SOLD sign sprouts in another American front yard.

My qualifications for writing a book directed at agents, sellers, and buyers are not limited to my longevity in the industry, although that is highly relevant to the success I've achieved in it. Also important are the specific skills I mastered over an extended period and the judgment I gradually acquired to deploy them to best advantage while serving clients. And then, naturally, there is my standing in the business. There are honors—for example, Rookie of the Year, Chairman's Circle, and Legend Award. Perhaps more important is my hard-earned reputation among my peers for having a reliable moral compass, which normally keeps me on the straight and narrow path of conscientious, good-natured, fair treatment of all parties with whom I interact in my professional life.

I am what's now called a solo practitioner, which was the fashion when I started out. These days many agents serve on teams, some large, which enables them to cite the group's impressive production figures on their professional correspondence. I have continued to go my own way because I long ago intuited that the kind of expertise and service *I* wanted to provide would require me to run a boutique business rather than a factory. Still, I have plenty of associates intimately caught up in my operation. The most important are my personal assistant, my mortgage consultant, and my tight-knit Business Family of top-notch contractors and specialized experts ready on short notice to investigate possible issues at houses I am in the process of listing or selling.

I confess that it has not been entirely smooth sailing for me these past several decades. The roughest part of my real estate career was at the outset, when I was transitioning from being an academic to becoming a Realtor. Born into a prominent dynasty of scientists, I had begun life as a scholar-in-the-making with this predictable result: UC Berkeley (BA), Johns Hopkins University (MA), Harvard University

(AM, PhD). After fourteen years of training, I had assumed the position of junior professor at Harvard and authored a major book for the Harvard University Press. My subject was a world-famous scholar (Wang Guowei, 1877-1927), whose collected works were all in Classical Chinese, which meant my research entailed nine years of deciphering murky, ancient-style Chinese texts. It was not until my first husband accepted a job far away from Harvard that I intuited my Sinological career as I knew it would soon be at risk. That led eventually to my unanticipated detour into the hurly-burly world of residential real estate.

Back in the rough-and-tumble days of my novitiate, the sales office I joined was unpromisingly located in the basement of a small business concern. To my naïve eyes, it appeared to be a den of vipers akin to the sales group in the movie *Glengarry Glen Ross.* Pugnacious agents vituperatively attacked one another. Our office administrator regularly made grown women cry with her incessantly sharp tongue. Our office secretary deployed the f-word so often and so loudly that making client calls from the building was out of the question. Well-meaning colleagues advised me to take my trash home in my briefcase to avoid having it picked over by the unscrupulous in search of leads to steal. "You can't be too careful," one of them whispered, "just look at what happened to Carol." Being new, I had no clue what had happened to Carol. My informant rolled her eyes. "A client called the office and asked for Carol. You-know-who was on desk duty and told Carol's client that Carol was no longer with our office and had left no forwarding number. You-know-who then sweetly inquired whether *she* could be of service to the caller."

My eventual answer to the seemingly messy, cutthroat nature of the world in which I now uncomfortably found myself was to aim high: I wanted to become a successful Realtor with a reputation for integrity. I wanted to demonstrate that a perfectly honest, straightforward, and transparent real estate agent was not an oxymoron. I'd make a serious living doing business not the wrong way but the right way, confirming through my career trajectory that there was no reason, no reason at all, for agents to steal others' leads, whether from trash cans or telephones or anywhere else.

This rookie's path thus diverged from You-know-who's right from the start. As for the modus operandi of my disingenuous colleague, I regret to state that it did not change over time. The woman enjoyed a flourishing business for many years with clients presumably as disagreeable and unprincipled as she. The fact of the matter, though, is that You-know-who left what Dr. Henry Cloud, in *Integrity: The Courage to Meet the Demands of Reality,* terms a "bad wake." So intense was the ill-will she created among the ranks of her fellow Realtors that when her car unexpectedly flipped over in a freak accident, maiming her, there was actual cheering in my office. It was uncharitable and in the poorest possible taste, but the schadenfreude was understandable given the accident victim's long history of extreme mean-temperedness.

The Big Boat

Over the years, I have come to regard my clients as cherished passengers in a Big Boat—*my* boat. The metaphor derives from an experience I had not long after my first husband and I moved from Cambridge, Massachusetts, to a distant city whose most prestigious university he had agreed to join as a senior administrator. Most unexpectedly, the two of us soon had the honor of being invited to accompany the university's president and his wife on an eighteen-day sojourn to Japan, Hong Kong, and China. In the months leading up to the trip, my then-spouse gradually became anxious about what his responsibilities would be in helping to plan our group's itinerary. A colleague named Koichi, who had quietly been placed in charge of the proceedings (accommodations, meals, meetings, diversions, and sightseeing), tried to assuage his fears. "Don't worry, Andy, you are in the Big Boat." Gradually it dawned on me what Koichi meant by this. The four of us were in expert hands and could trust him to deliver an amazing experience in the Far East.

It took a career change and extended time in the real estate business before I began to think of what I do with and for sellers and buyers as having affinities with what Koichi had done with and for the university's president, his wife, and us two young newcomers. Like Koichi, I am committed to giving those in my charge an experience as smooth, stress-free, transparent, educational, productive, and memorable as I possibly can. To achieve this superior result, I call on my entire suite of abilities: intellectual sophistication, analytical skills, judgment, ingenuity, persuasiveness, patience, persistence, grasp of construction issues, and stable of specialized detectives able to sniff out troubles at a property.

People comfortably settled in my Big Boat have a devoted shepherd tending to and protecting them. This does not relieve clients of the responsibility during a transaction to think for themselves, ask me questions and absorb the answers, read over contracts, remember to undertake post-settlement repairs identified as important during the home inspection process, and so on. They appreciate, however, that having a guardian Realtor looking over them—and their house, once they have one—carries some nice benefits. One is enjoying priority access to my nonpareil Business Family when they need contracting services, a landscaper, a waterproofing expert, or whatever else a homeowner might require: I have one of every type of house-related specialist in my "family." Besides doing outstanding work at fair prices, my "relatives" turn up on time, say please and thank you, clean up after themselves, and don't disappear until they finish the job. Owing to how close my relationships are with those in my professional network, I am even able in most emergencies to instantly produce a savior for homeowners in distress.

A task I particularly relish is serving my clientele as a sounding board. In a typical week, I might field calls about the advisability of buying a generator (yes, especially if the house is higher-end), installing solar panels (definitely not in my region, where they are considered aesthetically disfiguring), filing an assessment appeal (not unless you are significantly over-assessed), renovating the house versus moving (the latter, because most people want more space, not simply updated existing space), installing a pool (in the COVID-19 era, they are gaining traction). To keep in touch systematically with my wide circle of contacts, I send out periodic community and market updates as well as tips and advice relating to real estate, such as how to tell if your radon mitigation system is working properly and how often you should do a general inspection on your home to catch and nip emerging problems in the bud. For years I have enjoyed hosting brunches, dinners, Thanksgiving pie parties, Chinese New Year celebrations, neighborhood get-togethers, Business Family mixers, cocktail receptions, and formal salons for those in my sphere.

A disgruntled former buyer once accused me of being a transactional Realtor—that is, someone in the business merely to make a fast buck on a deal and then move on. I was stung. A transactional Realtor—*me?* I loved my clients and would do anything for them! I never quit working on their behalf just because we had completed the transaction; I just didn't—*did* I? To forestall a second accusation of post-settlement inattentiveness ever gusting my way, I launched my guardian campaign. Today I tell folks I will be their guardian Realtor for life. Since most clients these days are younger than I, the life in question is more likely than not to be my own, but so be it. I'll serve as long as I can serve, and I've invented multiple ways to do so.

Even if you are fortunate enough, as I am, to have a Big Boat to share, what I have learned over many years is that not everyone will be an excellent candidate to climb into it. Some sellers and buyers want to do things their own way when it comes to real estate—and probably a lot of other things too. This can lead them into all sorts of unproductive behaviors: grossly overpricing their home, lying by omission or commission on a Seller's Disclosure, refusing to get their financial capacity verified, disrupting a sale in progress with an unreasonable demand, not paying monies owed to those who have performed services for them, and so on. In general, I've concluded that if a person *says* he doesn't much need a Realtor—he can sell a house on his own and/or buy a house on his own—it's best to let him try to do so. And if a person *is* working with a Realtor but *acts* like he doesn't much need her, it's best for her to screw up her courage and fire the ingrate. Things won't get better with time.

As for those who are receptive to Realtors and appreciative of high-level, non-conflicted professional guidance in home selling, home buying, and home owning, there will always be space in Joey's Big Boat for them—that is, for *you*. Welcome aboard! Let us get started now on our sail together around the hidden world of residential real estate, which is normally as closed off to visitors as North Korea.

INTRODUCTION

THE PRINCIPLE OF VOLATILITY

By the second decade of a Realtor's career, patterns begin to emerge from the welter of details involved in all house sales. Rules of thumb, even real estate "laws," gradually become evident. In general, dots that once seemed totally unrelated to one another start to connect in interesting ways.

Altogether I have discerned TWELVE LAWS OF REAL ESTATE that, like so many islands in an archipelago, form an interconnected chain. The first law is foundational in that it defines the ostensibly calm waters through which we are navigating as being liable to sudden squalls and storms. Individual residential real estate transactions are, in a word, *touchy.* They are susceptible to blowing up with not too much provocation.

Day in and day out, year in and year out, I thus handle a volatile product. It is not a home's tangible components—its bricks and mortar—that pose a problem; they're nothing if not inert. It's the *intangibles* affecting a residential property that cause all the trouble— the intensely personal and all too often idiosyncratic assumptions of a vain seller, or the unrealistic expectations of a demanding buyer, or even the ineptitude, aggressiveness, or downright chicanery of a listing agent or a selling agent.

Do you remember the 1970s song that begins *"Feelings,* nothing more than *feelings…?"* Most real estate is about emotions. We agents endeavor to ground the process of selling and buying in facts, professional assessments based on those facts, industry best practices, long experience, and well-informed advice. But try as we might, we don't always succeed. Unexpectedly, someone will stake out a position based on feelings rather than expert counsel or even common sense, and it is always downhill from there.

Are you wondering what kinds of problems can crop up when a domicile—someone's current or prospective *castle*—is on the market? Below are several from my exhaustive mental catalog.

Idiosyncratic Seller Assumption: "A Wealthy Buyer Is a Cash Buyer"

One year I had the privilege of handling the sale of a large estate. The listing debuted at an asking price of $3,000,000 and soon received an offer of $2,500,000. My seller was comfortable with the proposed sales price but irate that the buyer's offer contained a financing contingency. "Joey," he vented, "no one at this level of home purchase should be getting a mortgage. I don't like it and won't sell unless that odious contingency gets removed."

It's hard to argue with a business titan. I had, of course, confirmed with the buyer's mortgage lender that he had verified our bidder's financial bona fides. She easily qualified to purchase a property at $2,500,000 and would have no difficulty securing the financing she sought. "There is virtually no risk to you," I told my client. My client wasn't listening to me, however. He simply could not warm up to the idea of a potential purchaser of his property getting a mortgage to help her do so. This is an instance of a very quirky idea starting to get in the way of an otherwise straightforward sale of bricks and mortar.

Upon looking into why the buyer wanted financing, I found a compelling storyline involving a bevy of dependent children. My seller did not care about the compelling storyline any more than he had cared about the lender's confirmation of the buyer's financial strength. After the buyer, predictably, withdrew her offer, she immediately purchased an even bigger and more expensive estate. It happened to be located directly across the street from our listing (ouch!). *That* seller had no problem accepting the offer of a well-qualified executive with a financing contingency. As for my team, we eventually found a second buyer, but my client's wacky thinking cost him a full half-million dollars because the second buyer would only pay $2,000,000 for the property.

This sort of thing happens much more than you might imagine.

Unrealistic Buyer Expectation: "He'll Throw in a New Water Heater"

In my sales region, Realtors generally follow a basic rule of thumb regarding an appliance or system in a house. If it is nearing the end of its useful life but still functioning properly, a buyer is not entitled to demand a new one from the seller.

Who determines the approximate age and condition of a home's components? It is the buyer's general inspector. He puts his findings in an official report, which is customarily used as a basis for any subsequent negotiations between the parties.

Now and again, a buyer will swim against the tide of local real estate practice, usually with poor results. My first-time buyer Sheila was such a one. In the end, her purchase of an attractive little assemblage of bricks and mortar was subverted by the headstrong position she took on a water heater.

The townhome I had secured at a favorable price for Sheila was only ten or twelve years old. If constructed properly, at that tender age it should not yet have developed any big issues, and my buyer's inspector found none. He did note in his report, though, that while the water heater was working well, it was nearing the end of its useful life and would require replacement in the not-too-distant future.

The fact that this inspection, unlike that performed for virtually every other home buyer on the planet, had turned up not a single problem did not impress Sheila. She was upset by the water heater's age and wanted to insist the seller install a new one prior to closing. After explaining the rule of thumb we agents use as a guide in negotiations over inspection findings, I expected my client to drop the matter. Instead, she doubled down on her position. Did she understand, I asked, that the seller's response to a demand for a new water heater would most likely be no? Did she really want to irritate the owner of the house she was endeavoring to buy over a $500 item (water heaters still cost $500 then)? She did! "Joey, I want a new water heater thrown into the deal. You are *my* Realtor, not the seller's, so get it for me."

Well, I tried like mad to get it for Sheila despite the unreasonableness of the request, but the seller's response was, predictably, no. The water heater worked "just fine," he said; the buyer's inspection report said so. Didn't my client and I know the rules of the real estate game? One of us did.

Sheila was livid upon being informed she could not wrest a new water heater out of the seller. I was unable to calm her down. "It's only $500," I soothed, "not too big an expense when the time comes, which could still be a way off." My buyer's response was to terminate the Agreement of Sale we had in place and to fire me for good measure.

Aggressive Agent: "The House Has *NO* Issues!"

My lovely relocating buyers the Andos became interested in a newer-construction manor home in a luxury community in the middle of my market area. The property, offered at $1,700,000, had been on the market for several months and faced competition from three other houses for sale within that specific enclave, not to mention competing houses outside of it. After touring the residence with my clients, I phoned the listing agent from the premises to express our general enthusiasm for the property. We did have one misgiving.

From the rear of the home's impressive center hall, French doors opened out onto a magnificent flagstone terrace. When we walked out onto it, though, the terrace proved not to be sitting on the ground! Because of the backyard's sloping terrain, it was sitting on a one-story-high addition to the house. The arrangement struck me as odd, so my buyers and I went down the exterior staircase on the side of the terrace to investigate the structure underneath.

"Bill," I said to my colleague over my iPhone, "that room underneath the terrace has a door that is unlocked, and we went in."

"So?"

"There was water dripping from the ceiling and down every wall in what is apparently an unfinished, clammy storage space. Also, we noticed a potential structural issue near the top of the external staircase—there were multiple cracks in the stucco. My clients wanted me to ask whether you think the sellers would work with us to figure out what's going on there in the event that we proceed to submit an offer. They *love* the property."

"You are not a home inspector, Joey, so *don't* go there."

"But..."

"For your information, the property has been pre-inspected, and the report states that the house has *NO* issues! That's just an outdoor storage space with a terrace on the top."

I pointed out to Bill that there was evidence of flooding in that storage area, which perhaps explained why nothing was stored in it. "We simply want to understand how bad the ongoing deterioration of the moist utility space is and figure out why the stucco underneath all that heavy flagstone lying on top of its roof is cracking."

I'd never known Bill to be anything but collegial. However, he now bellowed into my iPhone loud enough for my buyers to hear his response. "My sellers will not deal with this stuff, Joey, get it? You are totally off-base!"

"Let's not pursue this home anymore," Gabriella whispered, shaking her head. "It sounds like the owners would not be interested in working with us in a measured, cooperative way."

It is highly questionable whether, in his capacity as their listing agent, Bill should have intemperately spoken for his sellers without consulting them first to get *their* opinion on the matter at hand. *They* were the principals. After enduring several months of fruitlessly seeking a buyer and being faced with competing listings both inside and outside of their very upscale community, these homeowners probably would have welcomed the news that a highly qualified relocating couple was extremely interested in their home. Perhaps they would have responded reasonably to my clients' provisional concerns about the outdoor storage room's integrity by assuring them that they'd be open to discussing the findings of whatever professional home inspector the pair engaged to critique it. Because of Bill's emotional outburst, we'll never know.

"Feelings, nothing more than *feelings...* "

**LAW #1: "Selling and buying real property
is a *very* touchy business."**

Part One

DRAMATIS PERSONAE

(AGENT, SELLER, BUYER)

Chapter 1

FOR THE REALTOR IT'S SELL OR PERISH

As someone who grew up in an academic environment and enjoyed a first career as a scholar herself, I naturally am intimately acquainted with the ivory tower imperative to publish or perish. It did not take me long to discover that residential Realtors have their equivalent imperative. At first blush, the business seems easy. It's easy to sign up for real estate courses, which are intrinsically interesting and well worth taking even if you've no intention of ever selling any properties. It's easy to pass the state licensing exam. It's easy to find a brokerage company willing to take you on. The hard part comes next and lasts the entire length of your career: finding business. If you cannot find business and use that business to *build* a business, you are toast. The five-year attrition rate for new real estate agents, which according to the National Association of Realtors is up to 87 percent, is sky-high for this very reason.

When viewed from the bottom-line perspective of sales productivity, a Realtor's career is under perpetual assault by her numbers. If they are high enough, she is respected and well-compensated. If they're not, her commission split with her brokerage company may be adjusted downward, which is nothing if not downright disheartening to a hardworking practitioner. It is no wonder, then, that such a gigantic proportion of real estate books is devoted to sales productivity and the particular kind of mindset that stimulates it.

Sunday Open Houses

Without an established technique yet for reeling in business, the novice Realtor will follow tried-and-true traditional methods. For decades one such method has been to host Sunday open houses for established agents with too many listings to service without help. That the public instinctually feels home selling is a trickier business than home buying would seem to be corroborated by my discovery, early on, that new agents can find it challenging to entice homeowners to list with them right off the bat. Buyers, by contrast, blessedly have no reservations about working with Realtors possessing minimal experience. My first several sales were made to total strangers, people I had met while hosting Sunday open houses at colleagues' listings. It never occurred to these buyers to inquire how long I had been in the business, which may have been irresponsible of *them* but was most welcome to *me* at the time. We all have to start somewhere.

Hosting public open houses proved a fabulous initial way for me to solicit clients. Personally, I was never a fan of taking office phone duty, and today the internet ensures that the public will call far less than it will email anyway. Meeting people in the field, in an actual house, gives an agent a chance to size them up, chat them up, get their contact information, and follow up. With perseverance and a little luck, an agent will succeed in converting at least some of these leads into promising clients.

One of my very first $1,000,000 sales, back when $1,000,000 still bought a luxury property at a coveted address, was to a couple I had met in an unprepossessing home. I was hosting a Sunday open house for another Realtor, and Bob and Alice walked in the front door, lost and needing directions. I proceeded to give them—but not before securing the pair's full names and out-of-state home phone number. It was a good while before I managed to sell those two a house because they were initially constrained to work with an agent assigned by the relocation company managing their move. However, the agent proved not to be up to the job, and eventually (after much low-key, persistent lobbying on my part) I was invited to work with the new general counsel of a top Fortune 500 company and his wife.

Referral Pipelines

Besides hosting Sunday open houses to recruit prospective buyers, a newly minted Realtor needs to develop a dependable referral pipeline. No sooner did I receive my license, therefore, than I set about introducing or reintroducing myself to highly placed administrators and professors at the university that had lured my first husband and me to the area in which we now lived. It helped that my then-spouse was a senior administrator in one of the university's schools and that, through him, I had become acquainted with dozens of faculty and staff. It helped that for five years I had served as director of an East Asian interdisciplinary seminar series in another of the university's schools. Nonetheless, I secured as many appointments as I could with high-level administrators and department chairs throughout the university, whether I already knew them or not, to ensure that at least some of the top brass became aware of the unique new resource they now possessed: me.

My university referral pipeline would serve me well: I can count among my clientele top central university personnel, deans, deputy deans, department chairs, program directors, doctors, medical researchers, and untold numbers of faculty across the university's length and breadth. Many conceivable types of pipelines exist, of course. My partiality to mine stems from its suiting my academic temperament and scholarly background. What is *not* negotiable for a real estate agent is the necessity of building a pipeline that will dependably deliver seller and buyer prospects.

Professional Coaching

One year a senior executive at my company invited interested Realtors to take an extended bus ride with her to hear a presentation by "rags to riches" Irish immigrant Brian Buffini. For me, the experience was transformative. The next time the impressive trainer and coach of business professionals was scheduled to be in the area, very broadly construed, I made sure to attend his two-day conference.

The program was mystifyingly billed as a "Turning Point." Soon, though, I would learn that Brian's wife was a tall, willowy African American (he was short and solid by comparison), and that evidently the term alluded to the practice in the Black community of "jumping the broom" at a wedding. What a spectacular metaphor!

Picture in your mind's eye the device normally used for sweeping floors. There the thing lies, inertly, on the ground before you, representing, as it were, a turning point. Don't jump it and stay mired in the past. Jump it, as a bride and bridegroom might do at the conclusion of their marriage vows, and move into the future toward a hoped-for destination. There are no guarantees of success, but there is no going back. Symbolically you are Caesar and you have just crossed the Rubicon. Literally you are an agent embracing a unique opportunity to learn new ways to think about and grow your business.

As a motivational speaker with an international audience, Brian Buffini is peerless. His on-stage brilliance, wit, and wisdom are utterly dazzling. Even better, a Realtor cannot manage to forget the lessons he is conveying during a Turning Point program because the man has invented lead-generation systems, dialogues, real-estate related mailers, and other aids to help a salesman follow through on his principles and protocols. As an enthusiastic Buffini acolyte, I recommend a few high-energy conventions and podcasts starring this master motivator to any colleagues out there seeking insight into ways they might improve their outlook and grow their business at the same time.

Creative Initiatives

An integral part of building a real estate business is to try different things and see whether they work. When they don't, it is wise to refrain from doing them again. I was always big on having partners to cover territory unfamiliar to me. Mainly this was because my core constituency originally consisted of prospects the university wanted to hire. Because we have a wide range of outstanding residential options within a decent commute of the university, from the first I considered that happy circumstance a critical tool I could use in helping senior university personnel to achieve their hiring goals.

To take full advantage of it, I invented a service—Joey's Partners Program—to enable university recruiters to use me as a single point of contact when arranging residential overviews for candidates. Behind the scenes I'd set up tours in as many residential localities as the candidates were curious to explore—and I lined up specially recruited Realtor "partners" to help out by showing prospective new hires those areas that they knew intimately and I did not.

When low on clients, I would occasionally make an exception to this sensible system and personally take on assignments that plunged me into wholly alien territory. The worst faux pas I ever made by sallying into a locality I knew nothing about involved a family of six. Every weekend I would drive to their rental apartment, load everyone into my Mercedes, and set out on snowy roads for terra incognita. It was a grueling process, first educating the parents and grandparents (the grandparents had to be educated in Mandarin since they spoke no English) and then inducing them to zero in on a house to buy. Months passed. Finally, a listing in Pleasantville appealed to my clients, and we bought it.

Upon first touring the property, the wife had asked me about a big pole in the backyard (it resembled a tennis court light, but there was no tennis court). I had not then been able to tell her what it was, and the matter never came up again, even during my buyers' formal inspections of the property. Several weeks after settlement, the grandparents, who had endured the Japanese invasion of China during World War II, were home alone when sirens shrilly went off. The terrified couple sought safety by diving behind the living room sofa.

Lan shared this bizarre development with me later.

"Do you know what that pole in the backyard proved to be, Joey?"

"I can't begin to guess," I confessed, still totally baffled but grateful her tone was not rancorous.

"Well, it turns out that pole is part of a community-wide alarm system for the Lessing Generating Station's two nuclear reactors. They test the devices once a month on a regular schedule."

From the Zhengs' house—heck, from the whole town—any fool could espy the Lessing Generating Station's two cooling towers; they dominated the landscape at 550 feet tall apiece. But who knew that the communities surrounding the facility were required to install sirens—and test them either monthly or biannually? Not this fool.

I have never attempted to sell in Pleasantville, or anywhere else totally unknown to me, again.

**LAW #2: "Academics publish or perish;
Realtors sell or perish."**

Chapter 2

FOR THE SELLER IT'S CHALLENGING

For years it was a mystery to me why sellers so often cannot accept the value that live buyers in the marketplace put on their home, as evidenced by offers they perceive as "too low" or the lack of any offers at all over a protracted period. Listing Realtors know that some sellers can never be persuaded to take a first offer seriously if they deem it "too low." A second offer around the same proposed sales price, though, is highly suggestive (to the agent if not to her clients), and a third conclusively establishes that the sellers, not the bidding buyers, are living in la-la land. How did they wind up in la-la land? I think I finally understand.

A Unique Type of Artwork

Like artists, sellers of real property believe they have created something of uncommon value. They expect their new listing to generate instant interest among discerning buyers in the same way an artist throwing pots in his studio anticipates a warm reception once his meritorious offerings arrive in a gallery. A beautifully maintained residence with quality interior finishes and well-manicured grounds (perhaps boasting a pool or other sort of water feature) is, from this perspective, a one-of-a-kind metaphorical work of art.

It is this proprietary *feeling* about their "incomparable" property that causes home sellers so often to run amok during the publicized effort to identify a ready, willing, and able buyer for it. They resemble artists that become averse to criticism once their work leaves the studio for a gallery. However, in both cases, the creators' "art" is now in the public domain and, as such, is subject to public scrutiny. The sellers' castles are open to judgment, in other words—multiple judgments. Not all homeowners take the feedback well.

A Dangerous Misapprehension

The typical seller imagines he can determine or at least significantly impact his house's eventual sales price by setting its asking price. It is true that the seller starts the ball rolling by offering his property for sale. However, it is the *buyer* who stops the ball rolling by purchasing it. This is the harshest truth of residential sales for homeowners, and rare are those willing to look this truth straight in the eye. Instead, many will insist until the cows come home that their castle is worth what they say it is worth. Prospective home buyers, however, like prospective art buyers, are free to reject the creator-sellers' view of reality. If all prospective home buyers reject it, the listing will gradually grow stale and sit on the market, spinning its wheels. Then it will sit some more with no takers.

An Odd Artisanal Retreat

One year I met with a senior executive of one of the area's major financial institutions. The gentleman, who had been referred to me, was seeking my "creative thinking" about a property he and his wife had been trying unsuccessfully to sell for the past four years. Shortly after listing it, the couple had purchased and moved into a new residence, I learned. As a result, the executive and his spouse had been carrying an empty house at a cost of over $100,000 a year all this time, which was "debilitating." By degrees, they had lowered the listing's asking price from $1,799,000 to $1,200,000 but offers still eluded them. Their Realtor kept suggesting they "reduce the price," but they did not feel price was an issue. What, the gentleman wanted to know, was *my* analysis of the situation? What would *I* recommend they do?

This listing's problem was not hard to ascertain. Four years into its marketing campaign, it was still substantially overpriced relative to its merits and demerits, and the only people around who had not figured that out were its owners. Because they had had the one-of-a-kind artisanal retreat specially designed and built for *their* family, its singular peculiarities and eccentric features were completely lost on them. Clearly, the gentleman and his wife considered themselves artists who had crafted an exquisite artwork, one which should command a strong number in the marketplace.

I recommended a price adjustment to $999,000. Once this occurred, the property immediately found a buyer.

A Historic Fixer-Upper

Another curious case of wild overpricing that touched my life involved a house whose historical core dated back several centuries. The shabby residence, which was at the extreme of what Realtors euphemistically call "tired," fronted on a street that over three hundred years had evolved from a horse path into one of the area's busiest thorough-fares. Despite these drawbacks, the prospective seller was convinced the pedigreed property was worth $1,000,000. All but one of my five competitors for the listing dutifully submitted a Competitive Market Analysis suggesting an asking price in that neighborhood. The two of us dissenters, appreciating the home's functional obsolescence and unfortunate location, recommended pricing the property in the $600,000s. The Realtor who landed the account later told me her client wanted to list at $1,000,000 but that she had managed at the last minute to get the woman to agree to $950,000. This beat-up place sold in the low $600,000s, exactly where I predicted it would, two years and multiple price adjustments later.

As it happens, this home was purchased by buyers who fully appreciated its need for a comprehensive revisualization and total renovation. Through the grapevine I learned that they admirably accomplished these ambitious (and no doubt expensive) goals. If ever they decide to sell, there will still be the matter of the heavily trafficked road abutting the property's front lawn to discount for in their asking price.

"Buying Listings"

This might be an opportune moment to comment on the not unknown Realtor practice of buying listings—that is, knowingly and cavalierly telling sellers what they unrealistically want to hear on the pricing front for the express purpose of securing their accounts. This is arguably an exploitative phenomenon. After all, a Realtor is presumed to possess specialized knowledge and has the legal obligation to deploy it for the benefit of clients and prospective clients alike. Sharing one's honest pricing opinion with a homeowner would seem an integral part of that obligation.

An agent's life is messy, though, as I started to appreciate early in my career while learning how to manage a first-time buyer named George (his surname is lost to the sands of time). He and his fiancée rented in an apartment building in Charlton. That was out of my beat but not so far out that I wasn't willing to help them find a starter home in that area. George proved to need a lot of tutoring. I had never been totally at ease teaching Chinese history and literature to large classes at Harvard, but I discovered through this particular buyer that I did enjoy teaching individuals one-on-one, via extended tutorials, the ins and outs of the real estate game. George reacted very positively to my coaching sessions, which was most welcome because I had belatedly discovered that the man was given to sudden bouts of irritability.

Despite his mercurial temperament, I always treated George with deference and courtesy. My new client loved how much I listened, without criticism, to his views regarding house-hunting and much else besides. It seemed his fiancée did not approve of my kid-glove treatment of George, who by this point had possibly started comparing her unfavorably with me. Their spats increased, and I never did sell a starter house to the couple.

I mention the forbearing approach I adopted with George because it eventually blossomed into the rule I fashioned to guide me through the moral labyrinth of how to handle clients who entertain ideas that, professionally, I consider ill-advised. The rule is this: "Even when wrong, the client is always right in the end." By this I do not mean a Realtor is ever excused from her fiduciary duty to use her specialized knowledge to serve her clients' best interests. Few try harder than I to pry a prospective seller loose from a ridiculous contemplated asking price, for instance, or to dissuade a buyer from bidding on a so-called white elephant (a house that will be challenging to resell).

What my rule acknowledges is this fundamental truth: while I indeed possess expert knowledge and have an obligation to share it, it is the *client* who is doing the actual home selling or home purchasing.

I can try to talk someone out of taking an action I believe is ill-advised. If the attempt fails, I can reluctantly yield to the person's unreasonable wishes as a last resort, or I can walk away from an assignment if I believe assuming it will reflect negatively on my professional reputation. The *client* is always right, however, in the sense of needing to do *in the end* whatever he deems necessary to attain peace of mind. I have a cornucopia of stories involving this theme, because it is always a problem for a conscientious agent when a seller or buyer insists on calling the shots during a real estate project.

A Spacious Condo in a Premier Building

When interviewing for a listing one year, I discovered via the prospective sellers that my competitor was proposing a much higher asking price than I was. This time, fortunately for me, the higher-pricing Realtor did not obtain the listing; I did. The incident gave me new insight into the thorny problem, for a home seller, of distinguishing between sage pricing advice and wishful thinking.

The property in question was a capacious, extremely outdated, three-bedroom unit in a prestigious condominium building. My competitor had recommended an asking price of $525,000. Since this place was destined to become a gut job, I predicted that serious buyers would find fair market value to be in the $300,000–$350,000 range. I had thus recommended an asking price in the $300,000s—preferably not too high in the $300,000s.

"How can it be that your pricing opinion and that of the other agent differ so much?" the bemused wife inquired. It was a trenchant query, but I was not prepared to share with Mrs. Taylor my suspicion that the competition was trying to *buy* her listing. Instead, I explained that for years I had kept meticulous pricing records, and I offered to forward that data to her. "My listings are typically priced strategically going out of the gate, and I usually sell them from my first price tag, not infrequently in bidding wars. Sometimes I need one price reduction to effect a sale, but not often do I need more than one." I paused. "You show me a pricing record containing a lot of listings with four to seven price tags over a protracted period of time, and I'll show you a Realtor with no ability whatsoever to anticipate what actual buyers are going to be prepared to pay for specific properties and to price her inventory accordingly."

Mrs. Taylor surprised me. "Well, we like you as a person but prefer the other agent's suggested asking price. Could we list with you but price at her number?" I thought about it. The Taylors did not actually know either my competitor or me. From their perspective, I could as easily be underpricing the property as my colleague could be overpricing it. That moved me, and I signed on for the project. We went out of the gate at my competitor's price tag, reduced that price tag twice, and eventually sold for $325,000. The unnecessarily prolonged marketing period cost my sellers $30,000 in carrying costs, since they had been constrained to move into their new retirement community long before the now-vacant condo could find a buyer.

A Beautiful Home with Just One Problem

Toward the end of the 2002–2008 housing bubble, I sold a wealthy couple a luxury property with what Realtors euphemistically refer to as "potential." In retrospect, it was an expensive purchase because the market later crashed, but prices were what they were during that overheated period. My clients energetically set to work on improvements, both substantive and cosmetic. Since the wife had exquisite taste and the husband an inexhaustible supply of money, the resultant home was gorgeous, if still on the small side for the prestigious golf-course-abutting enclave in which it was nestled.

In the fullness of time the bubble burst, and home values declined significantly for a decade. Toward the end of that sorry stretch, my former clients announced they were ready to sell and invited me to list the residence. A crisis arose when Judy declared the property was worth $1,600,000; I had been thinking $1,000,000 ($1,100,000 at the absolute outside). Being a veteran Realtor with a reputation in the industry for strategic pricing, I was naturally more likely to be right than Judy. Indeed, the highest compliment I ever received in this challenging technical area was from the manager of one of my company's other offices: "When I was helping my nephew find a house, Joey, I told him we could assume that any listing of yours was priced right on the money."

Judy, however, did not care about my track record. To her, expertise was irrelevant, and "comps" (comparable sales) did not matter. The woman wanted what she wanted and refused to take no for an answer.

How could I give this imperious lady what she wanted? On the one hand, I was the person chanting that the client is always right in the end. On the other, I had vowed never to traduce a seller's best interests by cynically obeying a delusional pricing demand. I devised an ingenious solution, which, mercifully, Jack and Judy embraced and which I would commend to any colleagues who ever find themselves in a fix like mine. The listing initially debuted at my sellers' chosen asking price of $1,600,000, but—crucially—it debuted as a so-called quiet listing. A quiet listing is one that, while registered with the multiple listing service, does not actually appear anywhere online. That's what makes it "quiet."

The real estate agent in charge of a quiet listing exercises total control over how much market exposure it gets—a little or a lot. It is true that some Realtors abuse quiet listings, using them to try to snag a buyer themselves for the purpose of securing both the listing side *and* the selling side of the commission when the property settles. My goal with Judy and Jack's $1,600,000 quiet listing, however, was benign. I needed a little traffic through the house in order to obtain feedback to share with my clients, but I didn't want the property's availability to become generally known via the grapevine. My nervousness on this score stemmed from the fact that, as all agents know, a listing once stigmatized by a ludicrously high price tag has a devil of a time recovering. Most often, it won't recover.

From early spring through late fall, I circumspectly gained knowledge about what buyers and their agents thought of my new, quietly listed home and shared that intelligence with my clients. Everyone had the same reaction: "love the home but not at $1,600,000 or anything close to that." Thus ended our initial round of marketing.

The property re-debuted the following spring, this time as an active listing (meaning it was now in the public domain, available on internet sites) at $1,300,000. Fortunately, word had not leaked out about its earlier astronomical pricing, but even the revised price tag—again chosen by my sellers—failed to impress the buying public. The house *was* shown constantly: prospects descended on it like locusts. However, the current crop of purchasers liked the price tag of $1,300,000 no better than the previous year's crop had liked that of $1,600,000. After many heart-to-hearts with my perplexed clients, we adjusted our asking price again, to $1,150,000. Convinced this number would trigger a bidding war, Judy wanted to give buyers only three days to submit offers and to stipulate that bids had to be *over* $1,150,000.

It was a good thing I talked my sellers out of that misguided strategy, because the house continued to languish on the market for the rest of the year. During that period, another listing in the golf-course-abutting enclave, priced identically to theirs, sold for $1,000,000. This Jack and Judy seized on as proof that theirs should sell for at least $1,000,000 too. Now, I am not a fan of price-by-square-foot analysis (it leaves out too many variables, including condition, layout, and lot particulars), but I knew Judy was. The opportunity to raise her consciousness was too good to pass up.

Upon completing my comparative price-per-square-foot analyses on the two homes, I emailed my clients a report. In it I explained that the interior space of the much, much larger competitor to our listing was selling at $185 per square foot. Given their home's considerably smaller footprint and lack of a finished lower level, a hypothetical sales price of $1,000,000 would equate to $270 per square foot. The problem was obvious.

When sellers do not agree to bring down an overly aggressive asking price far enough, fast enough in the face of no offers or even nibbles, nothing happens. Then nothing happens some more.

"Why should we drop our price when no one is bidding?" Jack asked in frustration.

"That is precisely why!" I expostulated. "Despite dozens of showings over nearly two years, we're dead in the water because the spread between the asking price and what live buyers would be willing to pay is still too big."

"Oh." Jack looked dubious.

"Buyers don't bid if they expect they'll get a chilly reception. They'd rather wait for the price tag to drop within range of what they're prepared to offer—or simply move on and buy something else."

⚜

Winter arrived once again, and we withdrew the listing from the multiple listing service. Miraculously, around New Year's Day, I was presented with an offer anyway; it was in the lower $900,000s. Predictably, Judy and Jack were unhappy. But then, even more miraculously, I was able to coax a second offer out of another pair of buyers suddenly interested in the withdrawn listing. It, too, was in the lower $900,000s, which annoyed my clients no end.

Judy and Jack did not appreciate that a listing Realtor gets excited when she is in possession of multiple offers no matter how weak one or more of them may appear to her clients. There is a chance now for her to "work" the competing bids. In this case I had only two in hand, not six or seven, but two served beautifully for the purpose I had in mind. My goal was to sell the property within the range of estimated fair market value I had given my clients at the project's outset.

Because of the dueling offers, I was able to sell the home for $1,030,000. My clients still were not happy, but they took the deal. For an entire year afterward, the new owners complained to me repeatedly that I'd run circles around their agent to get them to raise their offer over $1,000,000, which they now claimed they should never have done. Meanwhile, Judy and Jack refused on the day of settlement to credit a small sum to their buyers at closing for legitimate problems discovered at the presettlement walk-through attended by the buyers, their agent, and me. As for post-settlement, I never heard from Jack and Judy again, presumably because they considered our sales price "too low."

A Place with Potential

So intent are most homeowners on getting what *they* think their house is worth that they completely overlook the matter of carrying costs and the time value of money. Awhile back I was asked by heirs to an estate to take over the marketing of their late father's home. Although they had originally invited me to interview for the listing the year before, the siblings had rejected my pricing advice in favor of that of another Realtor, to whom they then entrusted the project of marketing the property. Predictably (to me), the vacant home gained no traction at its grossly inflated price tag. Months and months unprofitably passed, which cost the estate roughly $60,000 in carrying costs.

"I should have listened to you last year," Mark conceded upon belatedly hiring me to sell the property. That normally would have been music to my ears, except that it rapidly became apparent Mark was not prepared to listen to me this year either—at least not initially.

Against my advice, we re-debuted the listing at a price tag still so significantly bloated it stood no chance of enticing a buyer to bid. This story has a happy ending because my clients gradually came to trust my professional judgment, which led them eventually to agree to reprice at a figure I knew live buyers would find too attractive to resist. Instantly a strong cash offer appeared, and we closed a sale without further ado. The spread between the original asking price (not mine) of just over $1,000,000 and the ultimate sales price of $660,000 was significant.

The Bottom Line

Will homeowners ever *learn the most important of all real estate laws?*

**LAW #3: "The seller may propose,
but it is the *buyer* who disposes."**

Chapter 3

FOR THE BUYER IT'S ALL ABOUT PRICE

You've doubtless heard people insist that, in real estate, it's all about "location, location, location." Location *is* an important variable, but transactions actually hinge on price—price *relative* to location and a host of other factors (topography, lot configuration, floor plan, condition, finishes, and so on). "Price, price, price" is thus, properly speaking, the most important catalyst in residential sales. No wonder Realtors harp on price so much!

Listings as Necessarily Depreciating Assets

The public harbors a suspicion that listing agents want to price "too low" to make a fast sale for their sellers and a quick buck for themselves. This is a total misreading of what drives the sales process and how truly responsible Realtors conduct themselves. Time is *never* on the side of sellers because a listing is, by its very nature, a depreciating asset. It is worth the most at the outset of the marketing process and progressively decreases in (perceived) value as days, weeks, and months pass without anyone stepping up to take the property off the sellers' hands. Buyers begin to wonder what's wrong with the listing. If there is an obvious drawback (say, the house sits high up on a steep hill or abuts a noisy expressway), they may hyper-focus on that undesirable feature, which is bad for the sellers and their listing agent. Typically, though, buyers place the blame in the right place: the asking price.

Conscientious Realtors don't want their sellers thrust into a downward spiral where they are chasing the market, trying to figure out how much and how frequently to drop their asking price in an attempt to reinvigorate a "stale" listing. In this type of agent's view, the better strategy is to anticipate what asking price will excite both industry practitioners and motivated buyers and to list at that number from the outset. Sellers taking this approach frequently find buyers in a timely way. They may also enjoy multiple bids, a dynamic that tends to drive the sales price up higher than it would otherwise have been while also improving the winning contract's terms and conditions.

It takes no skill to overprice a house. What takes skill is pricing a house at a number calculated to make buyers love it and bid on it rather than be unmoved by it and bid on something else. The seller who holds out for an agent that will price high does himself a disservice. It is not about what he or any other seller asks for his property; it's about what he fetches for it in the end. By avoiding what they see as the pitfall of *pricing* "too low" to begin with, the greedier sellers, ironically, by and large wind up *selling* below market.

The Ubiquity of Compromised Locations

Under the influence of the "location, location, location" mantra, I started my real estate career shocked by how compromised the bulk of my sales territory's inventory is when judged by this standard. Busy streets, which are literally everywhere, are only the tip of the iceberg when it comes to bad locations in my market area. Proximity to a highway would obviously be bad, and we have both a Pioneer Expressway and a Macintosh Route cacophonously threading through our suburbs. Backing up to train tracks would clearly be bad as well, yet we sport miles and miles of tracks in otherwise prime residential neighborhoods. Other undesirable locations would include those abutting a nonresidential operation of any type, whether school, hospital, or business. We have plenty of those too.

Imagine my surprise upon discovering, over time, that houses in compromised locations do sell. All that's required is to discount them enough to offset the drawback of their compromised location. That's all that is required for every other kind of drawback too. Realtors adjust for a property's drawbacks—*all* of them, not just the location-related—with *money*: by making the asking price lower than they would have otherwise.

The Lesson from Crestview Lane

That an outstanding location alone, without reference to other factors, can produce a strong sale is belied by an experience I had several years ago. Asked to list a substantial residence on Crestview Lane, one of my sales region's most desirable addresses, I spent days pondering what to propose as an asking price. The biggest and most impressive manses on this elegant one-block-long street historically have traded at lofty numbers. My listing-to-be, though, had several flaws I felt needed to be compensated for monetarily. One was an aesthetically unsuccessful two-story stucco extension to the original stone structure. Another problem arose from the fact that the house sat extremely far back on its lot out of deference, originally, to stately specimen trees that had long since died and gone to arboreal heaven. This left a commensurately shallow backyard, one lacking in any evergreens or fencing to screen it from the neighbors' driveway, rear façade, and rear terrace—not to mention the neighbors themselves. The floor plan was functionally obsolescent as well: the kitchen had deliberately been built small (for servant use), and the capacious family room my clients had added to their home's first floor was nowhere near it, as is preferred today. Still, this was Crestview Lane. What could I ask for a stone-and-stucco manse on *Crestview Lane*?

After taking its considerable assets into account and docking the property for its several drawbacks, I arrived at an asking price of $1,150,000. When the best pricing expert I know, an office mate of mine, came to my initial broker's open house, she quickly intuited what I had been through. "Joey, when I saw on the Hot Sheet that you had a new listing on Crestview for only $1,150,000, I have to tell you, I thought you were nuts. Really, I thought you were *nuts*." This gal never minced words. "But now that I've toured the house, I understand why your number is so low. It's a perfect price for this property."

Time would prove it wasn't quite perfect. Owing to lackluster buyer response to the listing, I felt constrained within a month of debuting it to recommend a price adjustment to $1,050,000. My sellers acceded to the suggestion, and we quickly found buyers at $1,000,000. I can imagine the purchasers' thought process. "How often can anyone sneak into a large, classic colonial on a street as prestigious as Crestview for only $1,000,000? So what if there are a few aesthetic, siting, and flow issues? We'll deal with that stuff later." The purchase was a good deal in these buyers' eyes, and those are the only ones that ever matter.

Raising a Stale Listing's Asking Price?

Given the critical role that pricing plays in getting houses sold, it is important for a seller *never, ever* to raise his asking price (an exception can be made for new homes still under construction). It seems like a no-brainer: if your place isn't selling, lower the price tag until it does. Some sellers, however, quixotically will insist on raising it instead.

At the end of this past winter, a seller of mine indulged in this crazy maneuver. In eight months, we'd not had even a nibble on the listing in question. "Why would you want to raise rather than lower its price tag?" I asked, mystified. With a straight face, my client replied that his earlier number was only good until the highly competitive spring market arrived! "We can do this, Joey, as I'm sure you appreciate, because of the strong selling season we're heading into." Homeowners (along with their listing agents) lose credibility in the marketplace when they elect to do dumb things. Raising the price tag on a listing that is already moribund is as dumb as dumb gets—no matter *when* a seller does it.

What about the propriety of raising the asking price after a seller has invested some money to spruce up the dated bathrooms in his dead-in-the-water listing? No, that's dumb too. That listing was busy not selling *before* the seller judiciously undertook to do some minor updating. After doing that work, a wise seller would *lower* the price tag, not *raise* it! How in the world is he ever going to motivate anyone to bid on the darn place otherwise?

Price *Adjustments*

Then we're agreed: except for new homes still under construction, asking prices should always move in a southerly direction. That is what price reductions do—except that Realtors don't call them that. We call them price *adjustments*. The word "reduction" connotes moving downward, which is, in fact, the pricing objective of a responsible agent whose listing is not selling. However, few sellers with an overpriced house languishing on the market are up for *reductions*. "Adjustment," on the other hand, implies getting in tune with the marketplace, and agents like to imagine that using this term takes a bit of the sting out of the proceedings.

But why are price tags on houses frequently so far out of line with where savvy buyers are going to be willing to bid that they require price adjustments anyway? There are several possibilities:

1) *Agent error:* Even a Realtor with an excellent reputation for pricing cannot invariably be right, and it is a relatively small percentage of professionals that excels in this area in any case.

2) *Agent strategy:* Some Realtors may favor pricing high and negotiating down from there when offers come in (if they do).

3) *Agent greed:* There is a persistent temptation in the industry knowingly to overprice houses, and when succumbed to it is known as "buying the listing."

4) *Seller error:* This refers to the nearly universal failure of homeowners to recognize the limitations of their own homes and hence to overvalue them. (By definition, drawbacks to a property that will negatively impact the buying public don't faze its sellers: they would never have purchased the property had they not been blind to them.)

5) *Seller strategy:* Some homeowners may favor pricing high and negotiating down from there when offers come in (if they do).

6) *Seller greed:* It is tempting to demand an exorbitant price for your property, and when succumbed to, it is known as, well, greed.

An Instance of Seller Error

A touching example of seller error involved a stone dwelling I listed on a popular little street within walking distance of Arlington's shops. Its owners had rebuffed my recommendation to have an up-front inspection performed on their home of four decades. The listing thus debuted at a price tag that did not remotely account for the building's multiple hidden defects. As for its visible defects, buyers did see those. "Too much work," "gut job," "total rehab" was the tenor of their hostile feedback. My sellers could not begin to grasp why the public thought the house needed work. To them, bless their hearts, it appeared "move-in ready."

This couple was not greedy, merely totally out of touch with the reality of what today's buyers expect in a home's floor plan and interior amenities. Offers piled up. In the end there were six, all within $10,000 of one another (which just goes to prove yet again that the market speaks whether or not sellers care to listen). I let the assorted buyers know that whoever was first to round up his offer to the next $100,000 "threshold" would win the property, and that's how I finally got my clients to execute a sales contract.

Many sellers are furious when their residence sells for less than they think is just. These people were refreshingly philosophical. "I would have liked to get more for the house, Joey," Mr. Locklear confided, "but I came to appreciate it just wasn't in the cards." I smiled beatifically at this man who understood one of the key secrets to living well: "Rather than fighting reality, you bowed to it—and quite graciously too. I admire that." I really *do* admire that.

A Case of Seller Greed

Seller greed is a different kettle of fish. It's associated, it seems to me, with an attitude of entitlement, arrogance, and presumption. ("Do it my way or it's the highway—for you.") My clients the Earles, head-strong as buyers, became utterly impossible as sellers of this unfortunate stripe. The house they had insisted on purchasing was what Realtors call a "white elephant," which is always a problem for me because I know how heavy the headwinds will be when it's eventually time to sell such a beast. This particular white elephant sat on a hill so high one had to park on the street in winter and climb up to the front yard via handrails. The first floor of the house was not at grade level but on what we would normally consider the second floor, making it necessary to ascend an exterior staircase to reach it. In architectural style, the residence was eclectic: somewhat contemporary but with Mediterranean flourishes that included an oversized pool that took up most of the courtyard around which the domicile was configured.

My clients had paid $1,150,000 for the unusual confection three or so years earlier, and they had since spent several hundred thousand dollars installing marble floors, a dazzling new gourmet kitchen, and an indoor/outdoor sound system. Now the couple was relocating for work and wished to list the property at $1,450,000. This price barely made sense mathematically and certainly not in any other way. For over a year I cranked out regular, data-driven intelligence reports on the competition, feedback from showing agents, and local market developments. The sellers were unmoved by the cautionary tale they told. I got fired. A new agent took my place in the Earles's lives and flailed away for months. To my surprise, I was then offered the listing back.

Captain Ahab had his white whale; I had my white elephant. What was needed was a strategic price tag if ever I was to have even a prayer of selling this behemoth. Desperate times calling as they do for desperate measures, I sat the Earles down one afternoon in their living room and read them the riot act. This took the form of sharing with them a cartoon from *The New Yorker* entitled "The Disillusionment Café."

Do you know this cartoon? Pictured is a middle-aged couple standing before the café's maître d'. He is addressing the expectant pair. "Sir, madam, I'm afraid I have some bad news. Your table isn't ready yet—and it never will be."

Meeting the Demands of Life

In the years since my confrontation with the defiantly intransigent Earles, I've had multiple occasions to cite the abovementioned cartoon to the intractably dug in. The lesson always hits home. Perhaps that is not as miraculous as it appears. To live well, you need to give up on things you "should" have had, "deserved" to have had, but did not get and are past getting now. To sell your house, you need to climb down from your high horse and settle for a sales price that is *achievable*. It is the difference between what Dr. Cloud calls an immature character that "asks life to meet his demands" and a mature character that "meets the demands of life."

Which brings us back around to the matter of price adjustments, of which, incidentally, I did obtain a healthy one from the Earles after they had time to process "The Disillusionment Café's" implications. A price adjustment cannot be small to be effective. It needs to be at least *one price point* below the current asking price to have any impact on the buying public. My clients' listing had debuted at a wildly untenable number and even now, toward the end of its second year of marketing, was still hopelessly overpriced at $1,100,000. In these circumstances, a token discount of $20,000 or $30,000 would have been worse than useless. The adjustment I proposed—to $999,000—was what we needed to gain traction in the marketplace. Once repriced, the property quickly went under contract.

The Materiality of *Significant* Price Adjustments

The importance of adjusting price tags by *one price point* (or more) when adjustments are called for applies to listings in all price ranges. Under $1,000,000, however, a price point is generally considered to be $50,000 rather than $100,000 (or more). One time I became concerned when a new listing of mine in a popular enclave did not instantly generate as much "buzz" and associated buyer interest as it should have. Admittedly, I had accepted the assignment of selling the home at an asking price that made me slightly uneasy. It so happened that this pair of clients of mine implicitly trusted Zillow's opinion of their residence's fair market value over my own. A "Zestimate," as

Zillow terms the type of valuation it offers, provides a sight-unseen calculation of a residential property's fair market value made by nameless individuals using a proprietary formula. As you might correctly infer, such valuations can be far from reliable, not that a wide swath of the public appreciates this.

After much discussion, I got my sellers down out of the $900,000s, where the Zestimate was, but had to settle for a debut asking price in the high rather than mid-$800,000s. After several weeks of marketing with no takers or even nibbles, I prudently recommended a price adjustment to $849,000, which is where I would have listed the property if given my druthers. Since that *still* did not do the trick after several more weeks of fruitless marketing, I painfully proposed a further reduction to $799,000. Instantly two offers materialized. After playing them off against one another, I closed a sale at $789,000. Do you remember the old saying, "When the student is ready, the teacher appears?" I would alter it in the context of real estate to this: "When the listing is priced right, buyers appear."

**LAW #4: "At the beginning, in the middle,
and at the end, it's always about price."**

Part Two

THE IMPLICATIONS OF WORKING AT RISK

(AGENT)

Chapter 4

FINANCIAL RISK

Reflecting on my career to date in residential real estate, I realize I've gradually grown adept at discerning what types of sellers and buyers will prove congenial to work with. Today if I'm given a referral to a homeowner who peremptorily announces he intends to price his property too high for the neighborhood or expects to receive a discounted commission rate, I know to drop him like a hot potato. An entitled person that grossly overvalues his property or commoditizes Realtors is simply not a client I find worth having, period. However, it wasn't always like this.

Because it wasn't always like this, I've had some real doozies of disappointments involving potential clients and actual clients. Years ago, an office mate overheard my end of an unpleasant phone conversation with an emotionally abusive seller I'd bent over backward for months trying to placate. Afterwards she confronted me.

"Why are you putting up with that jerk's criticisms, demands, and insults, Joey?"

"Because I am a divorcée and really, really need to earn money," I replied.

"No one needs money *that* badly, and you know it. Fire the sucker."

I didn't, though, so in the end, as often happens in this sort of dynamic, he fired *me*. It was just as well because by then I had figured out the man had deceived appraisers sent by the relocation company to value his property as part of a corporate buyout.

Compensation for Results (Only)

Like life insurance agents, of whom my dear Al. is one, Realtors work at financial risk—that is, we get paid for our results, not for our time and effort. If our invested time and effort produce a sale, we receive a commission check. If, for any of a thousand reasons, we don't go to settlement after a month or a year or three years or seven years of Herculean attempts to close a deal for a seller or a buyer, there is no paycheck. Given the nature of our compensation structure, real estate agents are nothing if not patient. However, those laboring assiduously in my particular vineyard up to seven days a week, including nights (especially in the summer, when it's light enough to show properties until 8:30 p.m.), look forward to getting paid *eventually.*

Avoiding Free-Spirited Consumers

It's important to get paid *eventually* when working on commission; it's the only way to stay in business. Recently I spent two hours in transit to and from a distant property newly referred clients had asked me to show them. Several days later the pair requested we meet at another distantly located property, but I was unavailable when they wished to see it. After my own appointment elsewhere, I phoned the listing agent to report I had buyers interested in a listing of hers. "The people you are describing sound like the couple who called me earlier today and to whom I've already shown the property. Joey, you should know I asked them outright if they were working with a Realtor. They said no."

Upon catching up with the husband and wife I had mistakenly assumed would already consider themselves loyal clients of mine, I discovered that they had no intention of working exclusively with me or any other agent. "We're opportunistic buyers," the wife declared. "We *use* Realtors. If you happen to show us a house we decide to buy, you'll make money off us. If someone else does, she'll make money off us." This may be a joyful approach to using real estate services from the perspective of a certain type of free-spirited consumer, but the odds against a particular agent's ever getting compensated for her efforts over an extended period make it a horrible proposition in the eyes of a real estate professional.

An Imperfect Hedge

One favorite hedge against *not* getting paid eventually is to work with our friends and those friends' referred relatives. This usually works well for me, but the technique is not foolproof. One painful episode I experienced involved a referred nephew and his spouse. That account ended for me in heartbreak along with no sale. While heartbreak is not good for anyone, it's especially hazardous for salespeople. Salespeople *always* need to keep up morale.

In the case of real estate projects involving relatives of friends, I do not ask new clients to execute up-front one of my company's formal Buyer's Agency Contracts. This document was invented for the purpose of having buyers pledge in writing to pay a specified commission to my brokerage if they purchase a home during the term of the contract, which is set at 180 days. Even though it is legally mandatory for Realtors to foist this document on prospective purchasers at our first substantive meeting with them, I have found people are wary of signing *anything* upon first meeting a real estate professional.

The contract *will* get executed by a buyer down the road—at the time he submits an offer on a property—because brokerage firms need proof in their corporate files that everything required by law to be in them is there. Whenever I prepare an offer for someone, I thus include the Buyer's Agency Contract in the package. However, I always write in that the agreement is voidable on *one day's* written notice. There is a sound, pro-buyer reason for this. In the unthinkable event that a client decides to fire me before the expiration of 180 days, my alteration makes it easy for him to do so. This in turn instantly releases him from the terms of our contract, with its *implied* financial obligation to my company. I say *implied* because the contract, in fact, provides *no* fee protection to agents, at least in my geographical territory, because brokerage companies around here do not legally pursue those who default on a written pledge to pay.

About six months into the house-hunting project with my friend's nephew and his wife, we found a property sufficiently alluring to bid on. I prepared the usual sheaf of documents—they included a Buyer's Agency Contract since at the point of sale, as I mentioned, this *has* to be executed—and forwarded them to the couple for execution electronically. Upon receiving the paperwork back, I was irritated to note that a signed Buyer's Agency Contract was missing. Assuming it was an oversight, I made a mental note to circle back around to my young clients later and get this document executed to complete the file.

In the end the purchase didn't work out. We went back to the drawing board for another period of months of house-hunting, at which point the nephew informed me he'd be tied up with work for the next two weeks. At the end of that period, I was just about to call to check in with him when my phone rang. "Hi, Joey. I've got good news and bad news. The good news is we've found a house. The bad news is you won't be getting paid since we're doing the deal privately."

This young man and his wife had just spent nine months with me touring and discussing houses. In endless tutorial sessions, both in my car and in listings of interest, the two had gradually morphed from naïve beginning home browsers into sophisticated, mature home buyers. And now the nephew deemed it fair to walk away? "We never signed a Buyer's Agency Contract with you and hence don't owe you a dime," my erstwhile client noted testily before hanging up.

I thought back to when we had submitted the offer on an attractive brick colonial the previous spring. It hit me only then: the nephew was an attorney—a litigator! He must have *deliberately* failed to execute the contract on that earlier occasion to forestall any allegation that he and his spouse were reneging on a written agreement to compensate my company in the event they eventually waltzed off and purchased a property without me. But since my emended contract is always voidable on a day's notice and Buyer's Agency Contracts are unenforceable anyway, the obligation to compensate a buyer's agent is not a legal one but a *moral* one. Therein lies the heartbreak in those instances where one's own clients do not act in an honorable fashion.

Postscript: My Faith in Buyers Restored

At the same time as I was working with my friend's young relatives, I was also helping a lovely pair of repeat buyers. Like the former, the latter had tried unsuccessfully to buy one house through me. Like the former, the latter eventually identified a relatively expensive, unlisted property to purchase. The couple *could* have made it a private transaction like my friend's relatives had just done. Instead, appreciating my service over many months, these clients involved me in the proceedings and paid my office its standard fee at closing. Coming on the heels of the debacle with my friend's family, those buyers' principled behavior I found deeply moving.

Realtors get paid out of the goodwill and sense of fair play of others much more than you may imagine.

Termination of Listing Contracts

In addition to losing out when our buyers fail to pay us a commission, Realtors lose out when our sellers terminate a listing contract with us and re-list with a competitor. I currently represent a property that in five months has received only *two* showings because my clients insisted on significantly overpricing it (unable to dissuade them from doing so, I reluctantly took the listing anyway due to our long friendship). Every other weekend for five months I've hosted a Sunday open house for the public without being able to identify a single serious prospect. This is an unpromising, indeed dangerous, trajectory for a listing to be on, and a conscientious agent knows she needs to speak up.

I spoke up, broaching with the homeowners the delicate matter of the extent to which the market was showing us we had overvalued the property. Peter's immediate response was to announce that he and his wife would be terminating the listing. Mind you, this man hitherto thought so highly of my expertise—I'd helped his family with two home purchases and one home sale thus far—that he'd penned an enthusiastic testimonial (it's displayed on my website). The only thing that has changed between the time we sold the former residence and today, as we endeavor to sell the current one, is the market. Sadly, Peter refuses to listen to it.

The Temptation to Cut Corners

You see why predicting with reasonable accuracy who will prove in the long haul to be a paying client is a valuable skill for a Realtor, working at risk, to possess. Being an independent contractor is much more expensive than the public imagines. We are responsible for our health insurance as well as for designing and regularly contributing to our retirement plan; there are no company subsidies. As novices in the industry, we may start small and inexpensively, needing only a good-looking car (preferably one that will hold six comfortably), a smartphone, and a laptop. From there, as our business grows, our expenses grow—at least they do if we want to deliver top advice, top services, and top amenities to our clientele. We feel increasing pressure to make potential sales actually close.

It is at this point that some Realtors begin to compromise the interests of their buyers and sellers in small and/or large ways for an unseemly reason: their own financial well-being. If you are house-hunting, you don't want to work with a real estate professional that is prepared to recommend mediocre inspectors to you, knowing full well they'll be easy on the house they're about to inspect. This shortcut helps that agent to close a sale but may create expensive problems and even lawsuits for her client post-settlement. You want your Realtor to work energetically to realize *your* objectives, not hers. You want to find someone whose moral compass is such that you can have confidence she is putting her expertise to work for *you*, placing your interests above all others, always. Then, assuming you have a moral compass too, you'll *want* to make sure your agent is paid, in full, at the end.

Predation from Fellow Realtors

It is not always our clients' behavior that prevents us from getting paid in the end, since the predatory actions of fellow Realtors play a role too. Probably there is nobody in my industry that has not attempted to help herself to a colleague's client; we're all human. Once an agent tried to pry a pair of challenging buyers away from me after we'd been collaborating intensively for an entire year and had three unsuccessful offers under our belts. Her ruse was that she knew of a great house for them, but it could only be purchased through her. Fortunately, the ruse didn't work. On my team's fourth attempt, we succeeded in landing a property.

There is an ironic sequel to this story. When, years later, the couple was ready to move on, I was asked to sell the house. For months I tried to broker a transaction, but no buyers would agree to pay what my sellers insisted on obtaining for the property. My young family decided to withdraw the listing from the marketplace and continue living in it. After another year or two, I was invited to re-list the property. The sellers told me, though, that another Realtor—one in my own office that I considered a trustworthy friend—had made prodigious efforts to persuade them to forget about me and go with her.

Perhaps my weirdest experience in the predatory Realtor category was one involving luxury buyers from out of state who had gotten interested in a particular manse on a highly coveted lane. At my clients' urgent request, my assistant and I spent untold hours researching how and where a pool could go on the slightly awkward corner lot. At length I concluded that we should reconsider our options by looking at new inventory as it became available. One day a seemingly promising property debuted, and I rushed out to preview it. To my astonishment, I found the relocating couple in the rear yard of this property eyeing its pool. Close by stood a colleague of mine, eyes downcast. Those buyers had been a personal referral to me by one of the deans of the university I so often serve, but that agent had somehow managed to pry them loose. "I knew they were working with someone else," she conceded when I confronted her later, "but I never asked who."

Balancing Things Out

You may wonder whether good clients that remain faithful to their Realtor and either sell or buy in a timely way subsidize, so to speak, that Realtor's longer, messier accounts. They do. For every straightforward, fast transaction an agent may have, there are probably a dozen or more that are fraught and slow. One cause is unrealistic sellers whose listings spend hundreds of days on the market and endure multiple price reductions before finally getting sold. Another cause is unrealistic or half-hearted buyers—tire kickers, the industry calls them—that look at dozens upon dozens of houses before finally choosing one to purchase (or not). As one buyer of this type explained to me after I helped him acquire a $1,500,000 property in a fitful eight-year search, "Since our current house is okay, we weren't all that motivated." Also being subsidized are those accounts on which the Realtor spent months or even years but did not succeed in getting paid a dime for her invested time and effort.

FSBOs

For-sale-by-owner domiciles can pose a unique payment challenge for a buyer's agent, which is why less experienced Realtors simply steer clear of them altogether. No problem arises when FSBOs, as these sellers are dubbed, are prepared to pay the buyer's side of the commission at closing (they're happy just to save the seller's side of it). Some, though, won't do that. In those cases, the buyer's agent needs to secure the indicated compensation from her clients. Not every Realtor is comfortable broaching such a ticklish matter since, historically speaking, buyers are accustomed to having someone else cover their brokerage expenses *for* them. Sometimes in this sort of tense situation, the buyers will abandon their Realtor and deal directly with the FSBO whose house they fancy. Even if they've signed a Buyer's Agency Contract, the document is (as I've explained) a paper tiger.

Personally, I've not found selling a for-sale-by-owner's property an insuperable hurdle. My favorite experience began when my buyers and I were disappointingly exiting a lackluster listing in an enclave of newer construction that we'd targeted. By chance we spotted a for-sale-by-owner sign in the front yard of a house across the street. I rushed over to investigate and wrangled us an invitation to tour the property on the spot. It was a great match for my clients, who were not put off by the prospect of paying their own brokerage fee since the homeowners adamantly declined to do so for them.

The sellers proved to be tough in negotiations with me about specific terms and conditions in our offer. I was still in their home, in the kitchen, at 2:00 a.m., determined not to leave the premises until the offer had metamorphosed into a fully executed Agreement of Sale. I'm glad I stayed as long as was needed to tie down this particular assemblage of bricks and mortar for my grateful clients; they are still in the house seventeen years later.

Discounted Commissions

Although price-fixing across brokerage companies is prohibited, each company is at liberty to set its own commission rates. My company's in-house rules legally oblige us to collect, from buyers, a commission equal to 3 percent of the sales price of the property they purchase if it sells for under $1,000,000 and 2.5 percent if it sells for $1,000,000 or more. For sellers, who by tradition cover their own brokerage fees *and* those of their buyers, the total commission outlay for those using my company's services is 6 percent or 5 percent, depending on their property's price point. This system helps individual agents affiliated with my company to stand firm against fee-cutting requests from prospective clients ("I cannot discount commission, sorry—this is simply my brokerage firm's fee structure").

Nevertheless, there are Realtors whose voracious appetite for sales leads them to discount the total commission commitment by particular sellers, usually in a not-too-flagrant way that they expect management to overlook. One technique is for a seller's agent to list a house worth $900,000 at $1,020,000 to qualify it for the 5 percent total company commission rate, then not revise that rate to 6 percent when the property is repriced below $1,000,000 or simply sells for less than $1,000,000. This means that a *buyer's* agent affiliated with my company has to dun *her* clients for the missing half-percent commission on her side of the transaction, per our Buyer's Agency Contract, if she wants to secure the 3 percent co-op fee to which the company is entitled.

Why would an illicitly discounting listing agent deliberately compromise her bottom line in this type of arrangement? The answer is simple: sales volume. A Realtor, especially a big producer, may choose to play the numbers. If she can enlarge her pool of sellers considerably by including in it those who outright refuse to pay full freight or just want "a deal," she can make up the lost income on her end by pumping out zillions of such discounted transactions. The buyer agents involved in those transactions may not be so fortunate, since serving buyer-clients is much more labor-intensive than serving seller-clients.

History has supposedly demonstrated that a real estate brokerage business needs to charge fees over a certain threshold to remain viable over an extended period (my company was founded in 1948). Nonetheless, there are competitors in my marketplace that either regularly or occasionally take listings at lower commission rates than we charge. A colleague in my office some years back actually left the company to work at a competitor precisely so she could have the freedom to discount commission if she so chose. "But why would you choose to do that, Jeanie?" I remember asking, disconcerted. "You're a really good agent. You don't *need* to discount!"

It bothers me that some Realtors are willing to agree up-front to accept less than the going rate for their services. I don't see why this doesn't bother the homeowners who hire them as well. To me, this kind of self-debasing behavior is an immediate tip-off that such an agent doesn't value her own expertise very highly (if she did, she'd expect to be compensated properly for it). What's more, she's playing into the hands of those who would commoditize us.

The Starbucks Analogy

Obviously, it's a boon to a home seller or home buyer to get real estate services at a lower price rather than a higher one *if* the quality of the services will be the same either way. But like professionals in any other industry, those in mine break down into categories: 10 percent top-flight, 10 percent abysmal, 20 percent pretty good, 20 percent pretty bad, and the remaining 40 percent serviceable. Convince people your skill set is out of the ordinary and your probity beyond question, and I believe savvy consumers of real estate services will be willing to pay according to the commission schedule of a stellar company like mine. On the other hand, if people see that you'll sacrifice *your* self-interest (getting a full commission at the end of an envisioned project), why should they not suspect you'll sacrifice as well, down the road, *their* self-interest (the highest possible sales price and best terms and conditions in the case of a seller, the fullest possible disclosure of a property's issues during the inspection process in the case of a buyer)?

At the end of the day, it is, or should be, about how much benefit clients derive from the expertise and services they receive. In my view, an outstanding Realtor is like a fine cup of Starbucks coffee. People will always pay Starbucks prices for a Starbucks beverage. You can't charge those prices, though, if what you're selling is going to taste like mud from a fast-food joint.

Clients Seeking "Relief"

There are multitudinous ways in which an agent's earnings can get jeopardized in the tumult of a real estate transaction. Many, as just described, are baked into the industry's unusual compensation structure. Others arise out of a sense of entitlement and lack of self-discipline on the part of home sellers and home buyers themselves. Some clients just have a way of becoming greedy when things aren't going well for them. They'll demand that their agent pay for the cost of a mold treatment when that's the last hurdle to getting a difficult listing sold. They'll ask her to purchase a home warranty for their buyers (if they're sellers) or themselves (if they're buyers). They'll invent any number of reasons their agent should pay for repairs around their own house.

One of my most egregious examples of this last-mentioned method involved a guy named Rob, who was getting divorced. His bad luck started, as it did for so much of America, at the height of the housing bubble, when Rob and his wife paid dearly for a quasi fixer-upper into which they then poured over $200,000 in repairs and renovations. The work was orchestrated from afar because Rob and his family had moved abroad for career reasons within months of settling on the property. By the time they returned, the bubble had burst, a recession had taken its place, and the marriage was kaput. They'd spent not a single night together in the house after all the improvements were completed.

The feedback on my new listing, which was being shown around the clock, was consistent. "There's too much work to do!" "The whole backyard is taken up by the pool!" Once the property was under contract at last, the deal almost blew up over the buyers' request for a big credit at settlement to cover the cost of remediating a litany of issues discovered by their inspectors.

Rob vehemently objected to the proposed credit. "We won't give these assholes a goddamn dime," he snarled. "We're selling them a house we invested $200,000 in, and they're getting it for less than we paid for it seven years ago. *Fuck* them!"

Patiently I explained the risk of giving up a bird in hand, noting that the same problems that were bothering these buyers would probably bother the next set as well.

"So either way you'll wind up paying a credit, Rob. Besides, I'm confident I can whittle down the size of this one to a manageable amount."

"I've got a better idea, Joey."

"Great. What is it?"

"We're taking a huge haircut here. I think the Realtors should share the pain. Everyone needs to give financially to get the deal done, including you and the other agent."

Sellers who take a "share the pain" approach to their difficulties evidently presume Realtors need the transaction to work out more than they do. The arrogance of this extortionist attitude takes my breath away. Rob's attitude was the opposite of the respectful, appreciative stance of a well-adjusted homeowner aware that his agent is doing all in her power to secure the best deal possible for him—the best deal *possible*, not the best deal *imaginable*.

It took me a while to talk Rob around. "I'm just not inclined to go forward, Joey. You've spouted a lot of rhetoric, but the bottom line is that we should not have to shoulder the financial burden of the welter of issues these buyers have found during their inspections." "Why not?" I silently challenged my client. "The issues were discovered at *your* house, not mine!"

**LAW #5: "To get paid what you're worth,
insist on getting paid what you're worth."**

Chapter 5

PHYSICAL RISK

Although it is not widely recognized, Realtors work at risk not only financially but also physically. Probably none among us has not received a phone call from a total stranger, chatted about one residential property or another, and arranged to meet said stranger at that property. We do this a fair amount, actually, which does not mean no dangers exist but merely that we unreflectively brave them.

An Instance of Lust

Sometimes this storyline is incited by simple lust. A man I had met in passing at one of my broker's open houses asked me to meet him at his nearby property, which I knew to be a luxury estate. He thought he might sell it. Such is an agent's insatiable appetite for listings that, without thinking, I said yes. Then I got to thinking. I was a newlywed and this seemed like an odd thing for a happily married woman (at last!) to do. My husband polled his buddies at his country club, and they agreed. I called the guy back and suggested we meet at a Starbucks rather than over champagne in his garden. It worked temporarily only. He continued to make it clear he desired me, and I made it clear I was not available. The $2,000,000 listing, predictably, went to someone else.

Encountering a Racist

Sometimes the price of meeting a stranger at a property is to endure his casually disclosed racist baggage, as happened to a colleague of mine. A man had called our office to see about getting a Realtor to show him properties. The fellow wanted to see a particular house, he told the agent on phone duty, and possibly others in the neighborhood as well, so long as she could assure him that no Blacks lived in the vicinity. Didn't that guy have a discomfiting surprise when my office mate, who is African American, met him at the specified property at the designated time? To the credit of both parties, the stranger proved not as racist in person as he had sounded over the phone, and my associate—a consummate professional—stuck with him long enough to make a sale.

Exhibiting Horrific Judgment

Meeting an avowed racist in the well-manicured front yard of a residence in a bustling part of the suburbs is one thing. What I did was quite another. Things started out, innocuously enough, with a phone inquiry. A total stranger had become convinced I was the perfect Realtor to list his property! What had convinced him? I wanted to know. Where was the property? After obtaining satisfactory enlightenment on these subjects, I agreed to drive out to Middlesex on a certain date, at a certain time, to meet the gentleman.

Normally I would have informed my husband where I was headed. I had planned to call him from the road on the way over but instead got bogged down in a cell phone conversation with a friend who lived in the vicinity of my destination. By the time I was done chatting with Aviva, it was too late to call Al. because I was nearly at the house.

Somehow the micro-neighborhood into which I had just driven had transmogrified from neat, petite homes like my friend's to dilapidated shacks you'd see in Appalachia. Unaware that any part of my sales territory could be this down and out, I was already in shock as I started down the seemingly endless driveway leading to the address I'd been given. Why, this place was not merely in the sticks; it was in the woods—*deep* in the woods. There was a menacing ravine a stone's throw from the house I was approaching. At least by this point, I could discern that the dwelling was new construction rather than another seedy shack. Still, I had not called my husband, I could not back out of that narrow and uncommonly long driveway, and now a male figure cloaked all in black had materialized and was standing expectantly at its top.

My mind was suddenly in overdrive. Panicked, it summoned to consciousness the story of Realtor Beverly Carter, forty-nine, who had been lured to a vacant home in Scott, Arkansas, by an opportunistic killer posing as a home buyer. Her body had later been discovered at a nearby concrete company at which the murderer had formerly worked. My body would not be found at a concrete company; it would be found lying at the bottom of a narrow, steep-sided valley well off the beaten path and deep in the woods. Curses on me for not letting anyone except Aviva know I was anywhere near this utterly remote, spooky spot.

By the time I exited my car, the figure in inky garb had been revealed to be a short, impassive fellow, and he had been joined in the driveway by a tall, threatening one. The former turned out to be the home's not-very-good builder, the latter its not-very-good financier. They weren't opportunistic killers posing as home sellers, fortunately. There was no way for me to help them unload the property, though; they were carrying too much debt relative to its probable fair market value for my company and me to make a dime off the place.

The Peril of Sunday Opens

An open house presents a special type of safety challenge for the Realtor hosting it. Usually, those coming to see a listing during a public event of this sort are a mix of curious neighbors, tire kickers, beginning buyers just starting to browse, mature buyers looking to buy, and (occasionally) mature homeowners covertly checking out potential listing agents for their property. Visitors that don't fit into any of these profiles are a problem.

Such a problem entered the front door of a listing of mine one Sunday afternoon while I was hosting a public open house. The property I was marketing, which belonged to two senior medical executives, consisted of a charming and spacious stone carriage house set high up a hill on an exceptionally private piece of ground. The only means of ingress and egress was a long, winding driveway. Our asking price was in the high $800,000s, which made me mildly suspicious when two young men, probably still in their twenties, turned up. What could they possibly want with my listing?

Since my guard was up, I remembered not to enter the basement before they did (this is a basic Realtor safety rule). In fact, I stayed perched at the top of the stairs to the basement, calling down to the youths to take a good, long look around. Upon resurfacing, they took a quick spin around the first floor and then headed up to the carriage home's second story. Something told me not to follow. No one was inside the dwelling but the three of us.

"Hey, you'll want to come up here," one of the unwelcome guests shouted down to me. *Want to bet?* "Did you know there's a dead bird in the master bathtub?" That was highly improbable—how could it have gotten in the sealed bathroom windows? "You really need to see this." *No, I really did not need to see it!* I knew the story of Lindsay Buziak, a twenty-four-year-old Realtor in Victoria, British Columbia. She had been killed in a second-floor bedroom of an empty executive house during a showing. Calling my office surreptitiously, I told the agent on floor duty I might be in trouble at an open house and asked her to please talk to me—and keep talking to me—until the oddball pair of visitors left the premises.

Meanwhile, the young men were now descending the stairs from the second floor, carrying with them a decent-sized dead bird! Had they brought it into the house themselves to plant somewhere to lure me into an ambush? "Yes, Marilyn," I declared, ignoring my guests, "that's very kind of you to look up that listing for me since you're in the office on desk duty anyway." I paused for a moment as the youths approached me. "I'll just stay on the line until you find the information I need," I said, brandishing my cell phone in the face of the two avian pallbearers.

Who knows whether these youths were truly bent on harming a Realtor? One convicted killer had this to say about the attraction of doing so: "She was just a woman that worked alone—a rich broker."

Intruder in a Vacant Listing

Entering a vacant home for any reason at all—and Realtors have dozens of legitimate reasons—is always potentially risky. I learned this early in my real estate career after another rookie and I jointly entered such a residence to preview it. Only later did the police belatedly inform us that someone else, probably a burglar, had also been in the house *with* us, screened from view.

At dusk one cold winter day years later, I drove up a long driveway to check on a listing of mine that was under contract and awaiting settlement. Since my sellers had already moved to a retirement community two hundred miles away, it was vacant. Someone had parked a truck out of sight on the grass behind the house. Lights were blazing and music was playing inside my listing! Without thinking, I dashed to the kitchen door and let myself in with the key in the lockbox.

"Whoever is here, I demand that you come out *immediately* from wherever you are and explain what's going on." My ferocity was on the order of that of a mama bear defending a cub. A man dressed in overalls slowly ascended the stairs from the basement. "What are you doing here?" I yelled.

"Calm down, lady," replied the stranger. "I'm the buyer's painter. He sent me to get a jump on things by doing some work before settlement."

"But that's not allowed," I spluttered. "You are trespassing and must leave immediately."

"OK, OK. Just let me pack up my stuff."

With the danger seemingly averted, curiosity got the better of me.

"I'm responsible for the security of this place. May I ask how on earth you've been getting into and out of it?" I knew it could not be by breaking into the lockbox because the device had been intact when I arrived on the scene and used it myself to get in via the kitchen door.

"Through the second-floor window that's only a foot or two from that big tree on the side of the house." The painter spoke matter-of-factly, with no trace of embarrassment, not to mention remorse.

"Oh, that's how," I murmured, struck by the devious man's ingenuity. "Of course."

Only much later did it sink in how imprudent I had been to throw caution to the wind and confront the intruder instead of simply calling the police to check things out *for* me.

Robbers at My Listing

Recently someone else broke into one of my vacant listings, this time via a small basement window. I was not inside the house but easily could have been. Instead, it was my Business Family's mold expert, about to commence a remediation project, who discovered we'd just had company.

> "There are muddy footprints on the basement floor, Joey, and it looks like someone cut and removed a lot of copper piping."
>
> "*What?*"
>
> "Yes. I think you'd better file a police report immediately. Also, send someone qualified to figure out whether these crooks turned off the gas when they turned off the water—I can't tell. If they didn't, the house could explode at any minute."

Since it was early Friday evening, I was lucky my Business Family's HVAC specialist was reachable and willing to send someone out pronto to check the gas. As for the rest, it wasn't easy to get the mold job done and also install new copper piping, a new boiler, and a new water heater all before settlement the following week. However, as my husband said approvingly at the time, "You got 'er done."

Harassment from a Colleague

Not all dangers in the field are posed by members of the public. Some arise from threatening behavior by someone in the real estate industry. Not every seller's agent, for instance, is a good sport about losing a listing to a colleague, and one time I was constrained to deal with an especially bad sport of this type.

Trouble started immediately. Since I was at the property the afternoon my sign vendor's big truck drove up, I had watched the installer unload my very substantial "For Sale" sign, dig appropriately sized holes, and firmly secure it in the ground. When I arrived the next morning for an appointment at my new listing, I was startled to notice that the sign had disappeared, never to be seen again. No Realtor that I knew of had *ever* had her big, expensive, personal signage stolen (as opposed to her small, unprepossessing company signs, which agents seem to consider fair game and are easily portable).

By considering motive (who in my sales territory could possibly have had one?), I provisionally concluded that the original seller's agent must be to blame. He had been furious at losing the listing to me. Perhaps he considered it payback to recruit someone to drive a large vehicle over to the property in the dead of night to spirit away my expensive signage. I reported the theft to the local police, then ordered a new sign installed. That too was dug out of the ground the very night it went in. I reported this vandalism to the police as well.

On his third trip in a week out to the property, my vendor found the replacement signage tossed in a nearby gully. He pulled the heavy, cumbersome thing out of the ravine and reinstalled it in the proper place. This time the sign stayed put, which was good since I'd only been willing to spend $1,000 on getting it to do so, and I was now approaching that sum. An office mate of mine proved to have buyers interested in the re-listed residence. Working collegially together, we soon got the property under contract to them. Then a scary thing happened.

Around ten o'clock one evening, my husband was driving home from a professional meeting in the city. Passing my vacant listing, he noticed lights on throughout the house. By the time Al. called to report this, he wasn't prepared to go back and check things out. I phoned the police, and they checked things out. Unfortunately, by the time officers arrived at the property, the invader had decamped, and most of the lights were off.

Who, I wondered, would have a motive for entering a vacant house late at night (there was nothing to steal)? And who would have known the lock on the living room slider had probably still not been fixed? I was starting to get frightened. Any day now I expected my tormenter to slash the tires of my car as it reposed in my office parking lot. Briefly I took comfort in the reflection that Al. and I live in a gated community with outstanding security. Then I remembered that, as a Realtor with former clients living alongside us within the enclave's gates, this crazy person could easily weasel a way in if he wanted to.

Jake never slashed my tires, and he never finagled his way past the security guard at my community's gatehouse (that I know of). What he did do was bring up at a regional sales meeting something funny he had witnessed recently: swarms of policemen descending on a local property. He had been on his way home from an engagement at the time, which was around 10:00 p.m. The sight of a squadron of police cars pulling up to one particular residence "caused me to pull my car over to the side of the road to watch the spectacle," Jake told the assembled agents and anyone else within earshot.

Ever since, I have avoided Jake like the plague.

Chapter 6

LEGAL RISK

To ensure that her clients do not sue anyone post-settlement, a *selling* agent needs to make certain her buyers discover any significant problems at their potential new castle during the all-important home inspection period. To prevent her clients from getting sued by anyone post-settlement, a *listing* agent needs to ensure that her sellers fully disclose, in writing, all known conditions at their property whether present or past. I have never had a buyer of mine sue anyone, and I have never had a seller of mine sued. That is not accidental. It takes a lot of effort for Realtors to set things up so there is no unhappiness on either the buying or the selling side *after* the parties have concluded the transaction and quit the settlement room.

A benefit of fastidiousness in this area is that it keeps agents out of legal trouble too.

Forestalling a Lawsuit over a Pool

A case in point involves former sellers of mine who deliberately with-held from me material information about their pool's condition, presumably to prevent the public from knowing about it. These home-owners had been FSBOs before being referred to me. Their house had been under contract briefly, but the buyers had walked away in a huff from the transaction after their inspections.

That seemed peculiar.

> "Why did they walk away in a huff?"
>
> "They demanded a large credit to fix the pool, but since nothing's wrong with it, we refused."
>
> "Oh, I thought since there's no water in the pool, something *might* be wrong with it."
>
> "We just don't enjoy swimming anymore, Joey, so there's no point in filling the thing."
>
> "Well, for marketing purposes, it would look suspicious to feature a pool without any water in it. I'm not sure that's good for the plaster, either. Did you ever obtain a professional evaluation of the pool?"
>
> "Someone did pop by to look it over, and he said everything was fine."

These new clients seemed to be holding something back. "If you don't mind, I'd like to call in a local pool company myself. It would be good for us to have on hand two kinds of quotes. One would show the cost of making any indicated repairs to the pool and then refilling it. The other would show the cost of eliminating the pool—in case some buyers would prefer to do that or it would be cheaper to do that."

I had a local pool expert at the property three days later.

"As I was telling prospective buyers for this place just a month ago, the pool is shot to hell. At this point, we'd need to start from scratch and install a new one."

"Wait a minute!" I cried. "You were here before?"

"Yes."

"Did the *homeowners* know you were here?"

"Yes."

"Was your analysis of the pool's condition shared with them?"

"Of course. The buyers were using it as the basis on which to request a big credit."

"Of course"—except that my sellers had deep-sixed the man's report and not bothered to tell me! I was having a providential encounter with the very pool expert that had critiqued the failed structure for the would-be private buyers.

What if I had not pursued the matter to get to the truth? Two disturbing scenarios sprang to mind. Under the first, new buyers put my new listing under contract and by chance engage the same pool authority as the original buyers had; it could easily happen because the town where this listing was located *is* a very tiny place. They thereby discover that my sellers had lied in representing the pool as being in serviceable condition. That could blow up the transaction.

Under the second scenario, the purchasers rely on the sellers' representations regarding the pool and do not bother to inspect it. When spring arrives, they engage someone to get the pool up and running. *Only then* does the couple learn the pool is "shot to hell." What a lulu of a lawsuit that would make—and I would be swept up in the litigation right along with my disingenuous sellers.

Fortunately, I was able to talk my clients around, ultimately prevailing on them to come clean on the Seller's Disclosure.

A House with Hazards

Even in an upscale neighborhood, dilapidated mansions rarely fetch into the $1,000,000s. When one did, I was puzzled. I had met the owners of the property several years earlier. As often happens in people's associations with a real estate agent, the subject of selling this couple's house "down the road" eventually surfaced. Since the pair had purchased it decades earlier as a "project," I recommended up-front inspections of the home's major systems. That would enable Ruth and James to know what issues, if any, the venerable structure might have. Afterward, they could decide whether to remove any of the revealed red flags (off-putting conditions from a buyer's perspective) *before* they started seriously thinking about selling their home.

I was at the house during its multiple inspections. In all my years of real estate practice, I have *never* seen a residence in such deplorable condition. Much of the century-old interior waste piping had failed, rendering most of the toilets unusable. There was no heat on the second or third floors. The roof was actively leaking in several spots, soaking piles of clothing stored in the attic. A particular third-floor room contained fungus (I took a photo since I had never seen fungus on an interior wall before, much less *red* fungus). Vermin had extensively damaged the top-floor windows and trim. The electrical system featured extensive knob-and-tube wiring, making the house uninsurable today (fire risk) without remediation. The owners' handyman (rather than a proper electrician) had done all indicated electrical jobs over the years, making an already unsafe situation even worse. The powder room's floor and walls were cracking, indicating a structural problem. The huge glass conservatory was on its last legs. The basement suffered from extensive moisture penetration and the mold that comes with that situation. This list is not exhaustive.

"Disclose, disclose, disclose" is a mantra drummed into Realtors from earliest training. "When in doubt, disclose anyway" is its corollary.

Buyers, it turns out, honestly don't care if there have been issues at a property they covet, especially if its sellers share what they did to fix them and provide the supporting paperwork. If they haven't fixed them, it's wise for sellers to present buyers with repair options and even quotes for the anticipated remedial projects. What is *dangerous* is for a seller *not* to disclose any "material defects"—this is a legal term—of which he is aware. If the buyer discovers them later, whether before or after settlement, there typically will be hell to pay.

This couple eventually sold the property "as is" through a colleague of mine that lived in the neighborhood. The purchasers were reportedly confident that a modest number of repairs costing a modest amount of money would bring the residence up to snuff. Based on my in-depth knowledge of the extent of the vintage home's issues, I cannot see how that could be remotely possible. Regardless, selling "as is" does *not* relieve homeowners of their legal duty to reveal what they know about material defects at the assemblage of bricks and mortar they wish to convey to another family.

Threatened Lawsuit

Despite a listing agent's best efforts, occasionally something untoward does happen post-settlement at a property she has represented. At least something untoward can happen in the *minds* of the home's new owners. That, let it be known, can cause almost as much commotion as a legitimate complaint.

The accusation came out of the blue in the form of an email from a long-ago buyer of a listing of mine.

> "We are very angry about a leak that your sellers clearly knew about but failed to disclose."
>
> "*What?*" I exclaimed out loud.

"You should know that hiding a defect rather than noting it on the Seller's Disclosure is not only dishonest but legally actionable."

Yes, I did know that.

The story related by the disgruntled homeowner was approximately this: the family had noticed a water mark on the ceiling below the shower in the third-floor bathroom as well as something happening to the paint in its vicinity. Their workmen had opened up the ceiling, which revealed a shoddy effort to patch a problem there. Then someone had painted over that section of the ceiling in what the aroused homeowner felt certain was a deliberate attempt to hide the leak.

Because of my clients' presumed malfeasance, the irate email writer now threw down the gauntlet. She demanded that the former owners accept responsibility and pay for the repairs needed to fix the leak properly or face a lawsuit. In addition, she was prepared to subpoena the records of all contractors who had worked on the home for my clients in the months leading up to my debut of the property as a new listing.

The facts as reported struck me as queer. Why, in the first place, would unhappy buyers wait several *years* to complain vigorously about a shower leak that, according to them, was already there at the point of sale? In the second place, the buyers had no need to subpoena any contractors' paperwork; they knew the name of the plumbing company that had done work at the house for my clients prior to our listing it. My understanding was that they had subsequently used that vendor themselves. Why didn't *they* just ask whether the company had ever worked on the shower in question?

When I had initially toured this residence, it was a sorry sight due to its lamentable condition. At my behest, the then-sellers undertook to install a new roof, new hookup to the public sewer, new plumbing for the three second-floor bathrooms, new moisture remediation system and mold abatement in the basement, and much more. My clients had mainly used members of my own Business Family to do the extensive repairs to the residence, and I could vouch for their integrity. Moreover, I had been on-site plenty myself during the house's six-month renovation and knew my clients to be doing a fastidious job of overseeing the work.

When I was a historian of China, I loved solving ancient intellectual riddles. As a Realtor, I love solving present-day real estate mysteries. What was the solution to the one now threatening to metastasize into a lawsuit against my clients?

My first sleuthing step was to consult those very clients; maybe they could shed light on the puzzling accusation. Bingo! "Never in all the years we lived in the house," Maya informed me, "did we experience a problem with the top-floor bath. However, we never once used it." My client's theory was that since the current owners' son lived on that floor, he was presumably using the formerly unused bathroom. If that were the case, Maya speculated, a condition that never manifested itself during their long tenure in the home must have now belatedly made itself known.

I wrote the lawsuit-threatening homeowner's erstwhile agent, requesting that she share my email with her client. In it, I explained what I had learned and shared Maya's opinion that the owners prior to her and her husband were given to making slipshod house repairs. "Could we possibly have a case of mistaken identity here?" I asked. Perhaps the current owners' reported discovery of a second-rate fix and a second-rate paint job to cover up that fix might be attributable to that earlier set of owners.

I went on to express incredulity at the suggestion that Maya and her husband, with whom I went all the way back to graduate school, would have made a misrepresentation on their Seller's Disclosure. "Maya is justifiably proud of the job she did renovating the residence," I wrote. "I know the lengths to which she went to bring the place up to snuff for a new set of owners. It is frankly inconceivable to me that, during this challenging project, my client and her workmen would not have repaired any issue they found at the third-floor shower along with everything else they were busily fixing—if they had been aware of one."

The email might have ended there, but as a Shakespeare aficionada, I could not resist citing one of my favorite tragedies. "It troubles me that your clients chose to go so long down the path of mistrust. Othello did likewise, eventually concluding Desdemona must have cuckolded him and therefore deserved death. In both your case and Othello's, the 'evidence' is open to interpretation, but the suspicious parties elect not even to consider an innocent one. Hopefully, your clients won't feel the need to follow the Moor's headstrong lead, which resulted in a pile of dead bodies on a bed. If only your clients had inquired earlier about this matter, I could have quickly obtained for them long ago the straightforward answer I'm giving you today."

I never heard from the current owners of my former listing or their agent again.

Widespread Wiring Fraud

Over the last quarter-century, many buyers, especially relocating ones, have gotten in the habit of wiring their initial deposits and settlement monies into escrow accounts maintained by the listing broker and the title company. Considering this practice benign—which it used to be—Realtors historically have thought nothing of emailing or faxing wiring instructions to their clients. But everything has changed now that fraudsters are impersonating agents, brokerage firms, and title companies so adroitly that monies intended for a real estate transaction are instead diverted into the pockets of crooks.

In response to this alarming threat that has developed, agents must now include an anti-fraud disclosure in the packet of documents every buyer must sign before submitting an offer. These days, my company has in place what it deems secure, if convoluted, protocols for wiring funds when buyers still wish to do so. According to my manager, the anti-fraud disclosure and new protocols arrived not a moment too soon. Prior to their introduction, we had in a single week three wire-fraud attempts *just in our own office.* Realtors were beginning to receive disturbing interoffice emails such as this one: "Today, a buyer represented by a company agent discovered he had wired $482,000 to a fraudster. A title company other than ours was handling the transaction, and the buyer believed he'd received an email from that other title company; it was actually from the fraudster. While efforts are being made to recover the funds, it seems unlikely."

In that instance, the money *was* eventually recovered. The kicker is that the buyer sued my company anyway on the theory he (the buyer) should have been warned up-front about the dangers involved in wiring funds today. The complainant has a point. We *should* tell our clients all known risks before they reach any real estate-related decision. Since we are the professionals, it is our duty to do so. In the case of wire fraud, we thus now include that one in the litany. If our clients nonetheless press forward, like hikers who ignore a Forest Service warning and proceed up a trail into known bear territory, well, at least they knowingly assumed the risk involved. One of the first things a Realtor learns in our business is that people differ vastly in their tolerance for assuming risk.

The Risk of Buying a House in a Pandemic

Despite the ongoing skyrocketing numbers of COVID-19 cases and deaths in the US, we've been enjoying an unexpectedly strong real estate market. Mark Allen of "Axios AM" memorably described it as the "new real-estate gold rush." I prefer to think of it as a new housing bubble, one that, if we're not careful, will burst eventually in the same disastrous fashion as the last one. That last one, you will recall, was not so very long ago.

Here in my bailiwick, listing inventory is consistently extremely low. Bidding wars reminiscent of the 2002–2008 era are back. Helping to fuel the overheated market is the sudden exodus from the city of those realizing they can attain a more congenial "pandemic-era lifestyle" in a spacious suburban home surrounded by fresh air and a lawn than by remaining cheek by jowl downtown in a condominium or townhouse.

I'd sold the home of a research scientist at a local medical institute after she accepted a position elsewhere in the country. When years later she decided to return to the area, Stacy asked me to help her find a replacement home. The one she wound up purchasing nicely met her most important needs, which were unusual. Nonetheless, post-settlement my client complained about the place a great deal, convinced that somewhere out there was a residence in her budget that would literally "have it *all.*" Thus began our five-year, time-consuming, quixotic quest for the perfect house.

Over that extended period, we visited and revisited any number of listings, spending at least an hour each time. One day Stacy contacted me, intent on seeing a certain property *immediately.* After her tour, my client announced she wished to submit an offer. Supposedly the bids were capped at five, which number the listing agent told me they had just reached. Knowing Stacy would have a fit, I talked my congenial colleague into allowing just one more. Then I spent most of the day ignoring an important luxury transaction in progress to oblige Stacy by preparing her paperwork and peppering the listing agent with questions whose answers I hoped would help make the offer irresistible. After submitting it, I waited expectantly to hear the verdict, which arrived that night.

Upon calling Stacy with the good news, I assumed she would be thrilled by her purchase and my fancy footwork in facilitating it. But something had snapped. Stacy now remembered that she had bad knees, making it imprudent to buy a house with a second-floor master bedroom (never mind that she lived now in such a house and just the previous year had bid on a residence that had a second-floor master bedroom). We talked about the knee replacements she might do sooner rather than later. There was plenty of space she could take over on this new abode's first floor to improvise a bedroom/bath she could use until her rehab following potential surgery was complete.

Getting more nervous by the minute, Stacy now also recalled that she was high-risk for COVID-19, just like me. But she had not been acting just like me, sheltering quietly in place. On the contrary, she'd originally gone to check out the new listing all by herself, waiting in a long line of consumers hoping to get inside the house (they had Realtors with them and could do so, but she did not and got turned away). My client had enjoyed a tour only the following day after I hired a young agent to take her in. I had temporarily marginalized a VIP's transaction to make every effort to help Stacy finally win her "forever home." But now that she had won it, her anxiety was increasing rather than decreasing. Our conversation proved short and tense. I concluded it by suggesting we both get a good night's sleep and talk again in the morning.

In the morning, Stacy asked me to unravel the deal because she absolutely could not change residences during a pandemic! This was nuts, given that it was she, not I, who had insisted on looking at and bidding on a new listing while a virulent virus stalked the globe. A sage Realtor once opined that this sort of equivocating client "will take a tremendous amount of your time and resources, and you will reach a point of total frustration" and need to fire her. I did, politely.

In all the years I'd known Stacy, I'd never realized she had an underlying autoimmune disease, which she revealed in justifying why she needed to get out of the transaction she'd originally been so gung-ho to conclude. Perhaps reality—*her* reality—did hit her in the face. Thinking through the implications of moving during a pandemic, perhaps she intuited that something injurious to her health could potentially occur. If that is so, my erstwhile client is like the hiker who ignores cautions and unwisely proceeds into bear country but turns around before anything horrific has happened. I do admire Stacy for *that*.

The Risk of Buying a Property with a Creek

We have been discussing risk—specifically the fact that people vary in their tolerance of it. Take listings with a creek in the front, side, or rear yard. Some buyers avoid them like the plague. Others are indifferent to the presence or absence of such a feature and, in cases where flood insurance is required, indifferent to its cost. Obtaining flood insurance *is* required whenever people get mortgages to help them buy a home in an officially designated high-risk flood zone.

Until relatively recently, there were seemingly no private insurers operating in my market area. Historically, the principal funder of flood insurance policies has been a program of the Federal Emergency Management Agency (FEMA), which is part of Homeland Security. FEMA's program is called the National Flood Insurance Program (NFIP), and it is available nationwide to all participating communities. To improve my understanding of how it works, I took two FEMA-sponsored virtual courses. From them, I learned that while flood insurance is a simple concept, the governmental program providing it is anything but that.

When people hear "flood insurance," they normally think of coastal states and sea-level rise. However, inland residential properties close to a river or even a creek need to be insured too, at least if their owners take out a mortgage. Because my sales territory is crisscrossed by streams, flood insurance is a familiar topic for agents working in the region. It is a tricky topic, though, because FEMA periodically *updates* its flood maps, which can adversely affect the cost of flood insurance for entire groups of homeowners. With increasing climate-induced flooding anticipated over the next decades, the cost of flood insurance will probably need to continue going up in response.

Besides the ominous climate trends that are increasing flood risks, flood insurance is a tricky topic because the national program funding it is in the red. Nearly a decade ago, Congress enacted the Biggert-Waters Flood Insurance Reform Act (BW-12) in response to that regrettable reality. BW-12 reauthorized the National Flood Insurance Program (NFIP) for five years on the condition that higher premiums would be phased in for designated groups of policyholders. In 2014, President Obama repealed and modified parts of BW-12, making a dense thicket of inscrutable regulations (and exceptions to regulations) downright impenetrable. Still, the general intent of the legislation was and remains clear: to improve the long-term sustainability of FEMA's program by selectively raising rates.

It behooves a *buyer's* agent to be proactive in investigating the flood insurance dynamics for any listing her clients love that might be in one of FEMA's high-risk flood zones. The first step is to ascertain that it *is* by checking the homeowners' Seller's Disclosure, by contacting her company's insurance affiliate for definitive information, and by requesting an Elevation Certificate from the listing agent. If the property *is* in a high-risk flood zone, this document will show what category of flood zone the listing is in and state what the home's elevation is relative to the area's base flood elevation (that influences the actual insurance rate).

Finally, a conscientious buyer's agent will *always* point out to her clients that, unlike mortgage rates, flood insurance rates are not fixed. They can and do rise over time.

**LAW #6: "To stay out of legal trouble,
learn the facts, and *disclose* them."**

Part Three

MAXIMIZING YOUR LISTING EXPERIENCE

(SELLER)

Chapter 7

PREPARE VIA THE "CHINESE TRIPOD" FORMULA

For a Realtor, it is exciting to be entrusted with the sale of someone's property. I care for my listings the way the wife of one of my husband's colleagues cares for her precious, donated kidney: with solicitude and gratitude. There is nothing I would not do for my sellers—except give them bad rather than good pricing advice, of course.

Eliminate Potential Issues

When I talk to prospective clients about my system for preparing a house for marketing, I liken it to a Chinese tripod resting on three supporting legs. The first leg of preparatory work is the preemptory elimination of so-called red flags. A red flag is anything inside a house or above, on, or in the ground associated with it that could alarm a potential purchaser. Ideally, a listing agent wants her sellers to remove obstacles of this type well before qualified buyers appear on the scene. The risk in not doing so is that they will freak out upon encountering one of them, and a possible sale may thereby be forfeited.

(a) Underground Storage Tanks

Underground storage tanks (USTs), particularly oil tanks, are an example of a red flag. In my region of the country, many homes are still heated by oil, and some of those homes continue to draw their fuel from tanks buried decades ago in the yard. In the residential real estate industry, we tend to experience sequential "fad" environmental issues: asbestos might be the red-hot problem for a while but then yield to radon, which might in turn yield to lead-based paint. In the 1990s, USTs became the red-hot problem. Eventually USTs yielded to mold. However, once the buying public gets worked up about an environmental issue, it is usually there to stay. I thus encourage prospective sellers with a buried oil tank to dig up the yard, extract the old receptacle, test for soil contaminants, re-seed the lawn, and install a brand-new tank in the basement.

The point is to get rid of red flags *before* the property gets listed, thereby keeping prospective buyers relaxed and calm once given the opportunity to tour it. Additionally, in the case of an untoward discovery—for example, contaminated soil in oil tank extractions— sellers will have time before the public sees the property to make contamination a nonissue by performing the indicated remediation. In my experience, buyers will charitably overlook a property's issues if they have been competently addressed (and there is written evidence of that); it's the *unaddressed* ones that cause all the trouble.

(b) Mold

Mold is a very conspicuous environmental issue today, one that, like a buried oil tank (especially if it is leaking), has the potential to subvert a sale. As such, this red flag is best eliminated up-front by a prudent seller. Of course, some mold so resembles dust that even a conscientious homeowner and an on-the-ball Realtor may not suspect any is around. This was the case with a listing of mine that recently went under contract. To my surprise, the buyer's home inspector discovered a small amount of innocuously presenting mold—it looked like a thin veneer of dust—on some objects in the basement storage room of my listing. Instantly I had my Business Family's mold expert run over, assess the damage, and give me a quote on what it would cost to do a proper remediation. My sellers even offered to do the work as soon as possible on behalf of the buyer. Then things got weird.

Katrina, the buyer, started to get fussy about who was going to do the mold remediation and who was going to retest the air quality upon completion of the work. Her agent explained that Katrina was injecting herself into our proposed process because she was "highly allergic to mold and had severe pulmonary issues." Given this new intelligence, my sellers and I decided we could avoid all potential complications by simply giving our buyer a credit at settlement in the amount of the combined costs of the mold job and the retest. That way, she could use my Business Family's expert and his retest service, or not, as she saw fit. Since we had been told the woman did not plan to take occupancy until she completed a slew of renovations, it would cause her no hardship to schedule the mold remediation for after closing along with the other jobs.

In recommending this tack to my sellers, I had in mind something I'd become aware of the previous year. In the pre-listing phase of prepping a home for marketing, I had suspected mold, summoned my mold guy, learned there *was* mold, and had him eliminate it before any buyers could come into contact with the house. I was in possession of paperwork showing the basement had contained slightly elevated levels of aspergillus and penicillium that had, however, been lowered to within an acceptable range. One afternoon I showed the property, now actively on the market, to an interested couple. The pair loved the house—until the wife opened the basement door and instantly choked up. It turned out she was *hyper*-allergic to even trace amounts of penicillium.

What if the buyer for my current listing proved to be ultra-sensitive to one or more types of mold too? If my clients performed a remediation on her behalf before settlement, who was to say she wouldn't hold them liable if she got sick—for any reason—after settlement? The woman was delicate and in questionable health by her own admission, with disclosed mold allergies and pulmonary problems. Doing work up-front for her would expose my clients to unnecessary risk ever after. My suspicions were heightened when I learned our buyer would terminate the transaction in progress *unless* my clients took the responsibility of doing the mold remediation for her. They no longer cared to, and Katrina terminated the sales contract. My sellers fixed the problem, the property went back on the market, and we quickly found new buyers with an offer only $5,000 below the original one.

(c) On-site Septic System Defects

For inexplicable reasons, some of my sales territory's most upscale residential properties are not connected to public sewer. Since buyers vastly prefer public sewer to an on-site septic system, it is never a good idea for sellers with the latter setup not to fix any known defects in theirs; that's a huge red flag. The whole purpose of a septic system, after all, is to treat household wastewater effectively and efficiently before it filters into the property owner's soil. If yours is not doing that, you are (pardon the expression) in deep doo-doo. Buyers will not want to join you there.

When Tim and Elizabeth asked me to sell their home, they mentioned that their service vendor had told them the septic tank was badly corroded and needed replacement. I quickly suggested we get their entire system checked out before actual buyers got anywhere near the place. The so-called load test did establish that the five-bedroom residence's on-site system was still capable of handling the amount of waste that such a large home is expected to produce. Nonetheless, a new septic tank was indeed needed, the sooner the better.

My clients, to whom I had sold the beautiful property a quarter-century earlier, resisted my advice that they immediately do this messy job—too much "hassle" involved. "But, guys," I cajoled, "you don't need buyers obsessing about whether it's worthwhile to take on a house where *they* will have to do the work of tearing up the yard, installing a new tank, and paying out of pocket for the privilege. You want to do the dirty job yourself ahead of time and present prospects with an alluring residence that's move-in ready." Tim and Elizabeth came around once they understood my rationale, and we got the job done quickly.

The new listing proved so hot that I called for offers on only the third day of showings. Five materialized, of which we took one that perfectly suited my sellers' needs. It was a cash offer and there would be no inspections because clearly the property was move-in ready.

Declutter and Stage

The second leg of seller preparatory work is making the house and grounds show to best advantage. Like emptying out and detailing a used car before advertising it for sale, carefully pruning back a home's furnishings and "staging" the property prior to marketing will increase its appeal as well as its sales price. I stumbled across the practice of home staging years ago when it was still essentially a California phenomenon. Sellers of mine had abruptly transferred to their new mega-mansion all the furniture in their old residence, and the interior of the latter (my listing) now looked terrible: without any furnishings, the eye was drawn unavoidably to the dinged walls, the scuffed staircases, the stained wall-to-wall carpeting, the uneven hardwood floor (a product of water damage). At my urging, the sellers engaged a professional home staging service. I was hooked.

Staging a house entirely with rented furniture and furnishings is costly, and I never recommend it except in extreme cases such as the one just described. However, every seller-to-be can benefit from the kind of inexpensive staging techniques that I have learned in classes and from affable staging professionals who have given me tips over the years. The most important trick in *my* kit is decluttering. People do not realize it, but they generally have too much stuff in their house. That's fine for day-to-day living, of course, but selling a house is an entirely different activity from living in it.

Typically, what is required to sell a house as fast as possible for as much money as possible (the two are related) is less stuff, usually much less stuff. "Declutter, declutter, declutter," I exhort clients. We'll walk through the house together, and I'll point out what needs to go. Once it is gone, I'll return and rearrange what's left, especially furniture, artwork, books, and decorative objects. I may suggest the clients repaint a room or two, remove dated wallpaper, set the table (permanently), dot the house with orchids, replace sturdy bathroom towels with delicate linens, buy a new bedspread with matching pillows. I do not neglect the exterior of the house. I may recommend that the clients mulch and weed garden beds, install planters on the front porch, restain the front door and polish its brass hardware, trim back or remove overgrown shrubs near the house, open the pool early.

You would be amazed at how far an energetic low-level staging campaign of this sort can take a homeowner. It absolutely reduces a listing's dreaded Days on Market (time is a listing's biggest enemy)! It absolutely results in a higher sales price than that homeowner would otherwise have obtained! Serving as broad a price range as I do, I would guess I've typically gotten my clients $20,000 to $200,000 extra dollars at settlement merely by taking the time (a few weeks to some months depending on the scale of the beautification effort) to make sure the property shows to maximum advantage for not too much of a monetary investment. I never recommend major facelifts on listings-to-be (recouping the investment is iffy), but I am all for minor nips and tucks.

Don't Commit a Common Seller Mistake

Occasionally a seller will decline to follow some of my presentation advice. Usually, it's because of an emotional attachment to how the house looks now, which is how the owner likes it. The problem is this: whether the house is vacant or still occupied by its owner, the over-riding goal is to effect a sale and move on. The place should therefore show to advantage from a *buyer's* perspective.

One of my current listings—it's a huge, tired, vacant mid-century contemporary—features a long pole (with wiring) dangling from the middle of the empty formal living room's vaulted ceiling. Gretchen has been an absentee owner for years but refuses to remove it. She has repeatedly insisted that the next buyer may also wish to use that space as a movie theater, and she's repeatedly urged me to include in promotional material the photo she shared of the space so set up. For purposes of *selling* a house, I have explained several times, it is always best to "show" its interior spaces the way most buyers would use them. "On the off chance the new owners might desire a home theater, they'd be far more likely to set it up in the family room or the recreation room than in the formal living room," I suggested. So far, my message about going with the majority's taste when marketing a residence has fallen on deaf ears.

Bold color themes in a house can turn prospects off. I once had a woman decline to rid her otherwise nicely furnished master bedroom of its oppressively blue cast. There were several large throw pillows, a bedspread, a settee, and two comfortably massive chairs all encased in cloth of various striking patterns—all involving white and vivid blue. The prospective client said she liked it that way, and *she* was the one that lived there. This lady was clearly not attuned to the object of the proposed exercise: to sell and *not* live there!

Another memorable account involved a completely mauve interior in a spacious, newer-construction brick home. There was mauve paint or mauve wallpaper on all the walls, mauve carpeting throughout the house, mauve bedspreads and sheets, towels, and toiletries. The mauve theme even extended to the artwork.

Predictably, the property languished on the market for months and months. One day, serendipitously, buyers materialized whose favorite color was mauve! They raved about the color scheme and quickly cut a deal with my sellers for both the house and $30,000 worth of its mauve trappings. They say there is a lid for every pot. The problem is the inefficiency in finding it when the pot's contours are too customized to take any but an equally and identically customized lid.

Price Realistically

The final leg of seller preparatory work is pricing the property. I cannot overemphasize how important the pricing component of a brand-new listing is. The truth is that once a homeowner has done all that is reasonable to do with respect to red flags and presentation, price is the only variable left in the equation for the listing's duration. No seller should screw up in this area right off the bat by racing out of the gate with what industry professionals and the buying public will consider a laughable asking price. The real estate community's initial impression of a new listing will be formed at its first broker's open house (or virtual open house), and that initial impression will incorporate what Realtors think of its price tag. It shows good judgment on a seller's part to do all he can to come up with a reasonably realistic one.

Otherwise, agents and buyers will find the new listing unexceptional at best and gross at worst. It's not the property itself, however, that is intrinsically unexceptional or gross; it's merely its merits and demerits *in relationship to* its asking price. At some lower price tag, Realtors would have formed a highly positive feeling about the listing, and buyers would have fallen over themselves to bid on it. In short, a seller and his agent need to put a strategic number on the brand-new listing at the get-go; nothing will happen, buyer-wise, until they do. Suffer short or suffer long, as my husband says.

An Instance of Unrealistic Pricing

The most overpriced property I ever took as a listing belonged to an exceptionally wealthy couple (they own a large financial institution). Had I not known Frank and Jane for years and years, I assure you I never would have undertaken to represent them. The couple was fully responsible for pricing the luxurious residence at $3,000,000, which was beyond excessive. However, the number proved nonnegotiable; Frank and Jane were "my way or the highway—for you" types. While they good-naturedly agreed to healthy price adjustments of $500,000 every half-year or so, we had started so high that the asking price didn't even approach fair market range until well into the second year of marketing. My clients cavalierly rejected their first offer and sold for considerably less when they accepted their second one in the low $1,000,000s.

Incidentally, although you may find this odd, I have long considered any property I list to be a bona fide client right along with that property's owners. I bleed for houses that get boos from the public because they are priced at, say, $850,000 when at $750,000 they would trigger cheers and, more to the point, offers. "It's not the house's fault," I want to cry. Unrealistic asking prices may be the fault of the seller(s), or they may be the fault of the listing agent. Either way, they are *never* the house's fault!

The Case for Pricing Strategically

In a normal market (as opposed to an infrequent housing bubble), much residential inventory does not sell immediately. When a newly listed property does quickly elicit a strong offer, the sellers' agent invariably takes it as welcome confirmation that her painstakingly worked-out pricing was spot-on, and she'll receive compliments on her perspicacity from colleagues. The sellers themselves, however, often see the matter differently, believing they must have underpriced their home for it to be bid on so fast. One client warned me straight out that if he got an offer quickly, he planned to turn it down. "But why would you want to do such a thing?" I asked, flabbergasted. "Because if I can get a good offer in a week, I must be able to get a great one in two or three weeks."

This gentleman's cavalier attitude toward a speedy offer has always reminded me of the joke about the four young friends in search of husbands. After gathering in the lobby of a hotel to which they've been invited to meet prospective spouses, they expectantly enter the elevator. Ascending one floor, the women see a sign outside the elevator doors: "The guys here are financial deadbeats, misogynists, and slovenly." Naturally, they don't exit the elevator. When they reach the next floor, a more promising sign greets them: "The males here are decent wage earners, treat women okay, and have average looks." The friends press the "up" button again. The sign now in front of them reads, "The gentlemen here are high-achieving professionals, deeply solicitous of females, and very handsome." The husband-seekers glance around at one another in the elevator. Then someone shouts, "But there's still one more floor to go!"

That "the first offer is the best offer" is a hoary real estate maxim. It *is* almost invariably the best offer for a simple reason: the only buyers in the market prepared to strike quickly—and aggressively—are highly motivated ones. Such house-hunters are seasoned: they know what they want and are ready to pounce if it materializes and is attractively priced.

It is a small miracle, really, the crafting of a well-informed, realistic, and motivated buyer. Over a period of months or even years, extensive work goes into educating an originally unknowledgeable individual in the fine points of home purchasing. Tutorials are conducted mainly in the cars of the agents who have taken them on as buyer-clients. Whereas beginning home shoppers merely browse, mature ones will actually buy—and buy *fast*.

There's often a backstory that helps to explain why a particular mature buyer pounces as speedily and aggressively as he does. Sometimes it's because he's already bid too low in one or more bidding wars and, having lost a house or two or three, doesn't want to risk losing another. Other times it's because the process has dragged on way too long and the buyer, sick of the extended ordeal, at last takes a deep breath and pulls the trigger. In either case, such an overripe buyer will strike the seller as having moved fast, but that's only because the buyer moved fast on *his* house! Overall, the buyer's pace has been glacial.

From working extensively with relocating individuals, I can testify that buyers of this type are also responsible for some quick sales. The local populace, whose members already have a roof over their heads, can take as long as they like to decide when and even whether to trade up, down, or sideways. By contrast, people who are moving for work need to find a domicile in a timely manner, get themselves and their family moved into it, start their new jobs, and enroll their kids in school. Their professional situation compels "relos," as they are dubbed, to see a raft of listings in rapid succession, learn a lot fast about the local market, and nail down a sales contract without further ado.

What this means is that any seller fortunate enough to have an attractive property, an attractive price tag, and an expeditious offer or offers should thank his lucky stars. He should *not* take the elevator to the top floor.

LAW #7: "The first offer is the best offer."

Chapter 8

EXECUTE WITH A SURE GRASP OF THE SALES PROCESS

M ost listings, unfortunately for the stressed homeowners involved, do not find purchasers overnight. Inevitably the question arises as to when a price adjustment might be in order. Figuring this out is a paramount duty of a listing Realtor. It is also an unhappy duty, since nobody likes to be the bearer of bad news and risk being killed as its messenger. In my own career, I carefully monitor both agent and buyer feedback from showings of each of my listings. I stay in touch with all showing agents over time to learn what houses their buyers are pursuing and putting under contract instead of the one I represent. If after a while (anywhere from two weeks to two months) there are no offers or even nibbles on a listing of mine, I get a pit in my stomach akin to Poe's tell-tale heart. A murder has not literally taken place yet, but it will; the pit in the stomach is my signal that it's time to kill my original price tag. That means it's time to raise the touchy topic of a price adjustment with my sellers.

Reprice One *Price Point* Downward (or More)

I've already explained that price adjustments have to be one full price point to be effective, but this bears repeating. Imagine for a moment that you are a buyer. If a listing you like gets reduced from $699,000 to $679,000, is that going to excite you—at all? What *will* grab your attention (and maybe inspire you to submit an offer) is seeing the price tag move from $699,000 to $649,000 or, better yet, $639,000.

An example of how efficiently a significant price adjustment can increase showings and catalyze an offer involves an exquisite listing of mine initially priced in the higher $1,000,000s. I was not positive we could reel in a higher $1,000,000s buyer, but I felt strongly that I owed it to my sellers and their exceptional home to try. The experiment was unsuccessful, which led me to suggest after a couple of months that we reprice. At $1,499,000, the property instantly captivated agents and buyers alike. The majestic stone manse, which had been renovated and expanded to marry newly created informal living spaces to the elegant, formal floor plan of the original structure, promptly elicited an offer *higher* than our revised asking price.

If you are wondering why I recommended $1,499,000 instead of $1,500,000, it's for the same reason merchants advertise widgets for $2.99 rather than $3.00: it looks better to *buyers* if things are priced just under what Realtors call a "threshold" rather than right on one or, heaven forbid, slightly over one. That is why, if an experienced agent has her druthers, she will price a property at, say, $799,000 rather than $800,000—and never at $815,000.

Verify the Buyer's Financial Strength

Once a house on the market is repriced strategically enough to elicit an offer from a buyer, the listing Realtor will quickly review that offer's proposed sales price as well as all terms and conditions. Assuming she takes her fiduciary responsibilities to her seller seriously, the listing agent will also obtain verification of the prospective buyer's financial bona fides. I have long been bothered by those colleagues who are indifferent to establishing up-front whether those submitting offers on their listings truly possess the wherewithal to purchase them. "Back on the market because the buyer's mortgage fell through!" they'll trumpet in a voice mail or email blast. It is disgraceful for a listing agent to tie up a property contractually in a deal that will ultimately fall apart over the potential purchaser's underlying financial inadequacy. It is easy enough to establish how strong any buyer is *before* allowing a seller to execute an offer from him, so why not act responsibly and make the phone calls and crunch the numbers to do so?

Understand the Inspection Contingency (Part One)

After any preliminary negotiations are successfully concluded and an Agreement of Sale is formally executed by the parties, the buyer will have a period of days in which to perform inspections of the property. The basic ones in my market area are a general inspection, a pest inspection, and a radon inspection. If the house's cladding system is stucco, the buyer's Realtor may also recommend that it be tested, especially if the house is younger rather than older. A swimming pool or tennis court usually requires a specialized critique. So does an on-site septic system, a private well, or a forest of cracked interior soil pipes. Other experts may be summoned if the general inspector sounds an alarm. The most common alarms involve suspected structural failure, environmental issues, moisture-related problems (whether inside or outside the residential structure itself), roofing/chimney deficiencies, and electrical hazards.

Stay Away during Your Home's Inspections

Because buyers experience elevated stress during home inspections, I always enjoin my sellers to stay away from the house until they are over. Once I had clients who returned to their handsome, newer-construction residence just as the general inspector was finishing up. The buyers, their agent, and I were in the kitchen. My colleague announced that the inspection had gone wonderfully well, which did not surprise me since the house's builder enjoyed a stellar reputation. To celebrate, the sellers made coffee for everyone.

Suddenly the general inspector sailed in from the yard, declaring that he had just uncovered an issue with the foundation. Inexplicably, one of my sellers blurted out, "Well, it's not our problem anymore." Want to bet? The buyers became so irate they relinquished their coffee cups, stormed out the door, and terminated the transaction forthwith.

It was late fall when this sale fell apart, and my clients were imminently relocating to a distant part of the country. They dreaded carrying the vacant property through a harsh winter once they were no longer around personally to check on it. Scrambling, I managed to find a second set of buyers for the property, but the sales price was somewhat under $1,000,000 rather than comfortably over it. There was, by the way, nothing wrong with the house's foundation. But by the time I could establish this, the original buyers were long gone.

Instruct Your Agent to Attend the Inspections

Some agents make a point of not attending any home inspections at a listing they represent, evidently on the theory that if they do not learn what the issues are at the property, they cannot be held legally responsible for not disclosing them to others later. In the event a sale falls through owing to inspection findings, such agents imagine this technique relieves them of the obligation to share with new prospective buyers what was previously uncovered about the residence's condition. This is simplistic—indeed disingenuous—thinking, and it can cost their sellers (and themselves) a lawsuit down the road. In real estate, ignorance is not necessarily bliss.

Understanding that she is accountable to clients, a mature listing agent makes a *point* of attending inspections being conducted at any property she is marketing. As the absent sellers' eyes and ears, she *wants* to know what the buyers' experts' opinions are on a variety of specialized topics so she can explain them to her clients. To process what she's hearing, the listing Realtor will necessarily have to possess a decent grounding in residential construction, understand the types of damage that can occur to a building (and the land it sits on), and have experts of her own on tap willing to do instant analyses of alleged material defects. It is a feature of real estate transactions that most every house, from the modest to the mighty, has issues, some serious; a Realtor without sophisticated skills in this area and a host of specialists up her sleeve is like a whale without a blowhole.

A responsible seller's agent wants to *make* deals, not forfeit them. That is why she attends inspections conducted at her listings and learns everything there is to learn from them. That is why, in some cases, she brings in experts of her own to assess issues identified by the buyer's inspectors. Most crucially, she explains to her clients that the bad news is *real*—that, for instance, she *saw* the five structurally unsound basement joists and the back-drafting water heater—and advises against disputing these findings if they want to sell; she gently points out that if this deal goes south, the next inspector for a new set of buyers will most likely uncover the same issues as the original one did. If the buyers have overreached in some of their demands, she can recommend that her clients ignore the gratuitous ones. I recently advised a luxury seller of mine to ignore a bevy of indiscriminate buyer demands, offer the would-be purchasers a lump sum, and be done with it. The strategy worked.

Understand the Inspection Contingency (Part Two)

After the multitudinous buyer-instigated inspections and follow-up investigations have been completed (typically within ten days in my market territory), the buyer will submit a formal Reply to Inspections to the seller. In response to the revealed findings, the Reply will state what the buyer deems it equitable for the seller to do to keep the buyer in the deal and moving forward. Usually, it is to give the buyer a credit for or toward any indicated repairs. Sometimes, though, it is to make specified repairs on behalf of the buyer prior to closing.

As a rule, it is better for a seller to give credits than to make repairs. Doing any work at all opens the door to arguments between the parties about its quality. Sellers and buyers have different objectives when it comes to remedial projects done in response to inspection findings. A seller's interest is to provide modest repairs and get out of Dodge. A buyer's interest is to obtain quality repairs that will prove durable. Because quality fixes invariably cost more than modest fixes, the best way to handle them is not to attempt any. Give some money at settlement instead. The buyer can use it to do repairs any way he wants after the closing is safely concluded.

Negotiate *with Care* the Buyer's Requests

When a seller takes an unreasonable position in negotiations over home inspection findings, it is up to the listing agent to bring that seller around to a reasonable one, thereby ensuring the transaction will progress rather than blow up. Last year I worked with a pair of gentle, straight-arrow, first-time buyers who elected to bid on an attractive stucco colonial in a popular enclave. On close inspection, the home proved to have multiple issues—more than the normal first-time buyer (or any buyer, really) could be expected to stomach. However, all the issues could be fixed, and six different specialists from my Business

Family quoted exact prices for fixing them. The total tab was $35,000, and my clients were amenable to staying in the transaction so long as they received at closing a credit from the seller sufficient to pay for the remedial work. Being a veteran in the industry, the listing agent knew—or should have known—what was now needed on her end of the negotiations to keep the deal on track.

The deal did not stay on track. It derailed because, with or without the listing agent's blessing, the seller offered a mere trifle of a credit. Instantly alienated, my buyers angrily exercised their option unilaterally to rescind the Agreement of Sale under the provisions of the Home Inspection Contingency. My clients and I renewed our house search and, in the fullness of time, landed a much more substantial and expensive home, which had the extra benefit of being in excellent condition.

Meanwhile, the listing agent of the problem-laden house kept asking me why my buyers had walked away from the transaction when her seller's offer was only an "opening gambit." This experienced listing agent of a compromised dwelling did not appreciate that a seller proffering an insultingly low credit for repairs might not *get* a chance to improve on his opening gambit?

Beware of Unrecorded Mortgage Payoffs

Once a buyer's home-inspection-related requests and the seller's response to them are negotiated to a successful conclusion, most listing Realtors consider the sale solid enough to install a SOLD sign on the property. Now there are only a few miscellaneous matters left before it is time for everyone to convene at the settlement table. The principal ones are cleaning up any issues the Title Report might reveal and securing the mortgage commitment.

A problem for homeowners that will be revealed (if it exists) in the buyer-ordered Title Report on their property is unrecorded mortgage payoffs. The more times the seller has refinanced his house over the years to take advantage of declining interest rates, the more likely it will be that one of the mortgage payoffs may not have been recorded at the courthouse. If that has happened somewhere along the line, there will be no legal proof that the homeowner in question paid off a particular earlier loan before taking out a new one. This is an unacceptable situation from a title company's perspective.

I learned just how much title companies hate unrecorded mortgage payoffs when I sold the colonial in which I had resided for the previous twenty-seven years. Over that extended period, rates had dropped from 16 percent to 13 percent to below 10 percent, and I had refinanced my mortgage multiple times in response to the declining cost of borrowing. Imagine my surprise at learning shortly before settlement that the paperwork for one of these long-ago refinances had never been filed at the courthouse. At the time I had no idea that it is the *mortgage company* that does the recording—or not. I learned the hard way that only the *homeowner* suffers if a mortgage company is revealed to have been negligent.

Because of my unfortunate experience, I knew just what to do when a Title Report on the property of a recent seller of mine noted that he had an unrecorded mortgage payoff from years earlier. I was able to resolve the matter satisfactorily without too much trouble and expense on his part. In my own drastically more complicated case, however, the negligent mortgage company proved to have long since gone out of business. What to do? I hired my Business Family's dazzling real estate attorney to figure that out, since my nerves were beyond frayed. I, of all people, might not be able to deliver clear title to my own home?! It was unthinkable. My lawyer eventually struck a deal with the title company wherein, as I recall, I had to pledge funds from one of my Vanguard accounts to cover the entire amount of that long-ago loan if it ever surfaced as a problem for anyone.

Be Alert to a Possible Buyer Default

Eventually, the day of settlement arrives. There are occasions, however, when not everyone turns up for it. This unhappy scenario accounts for the venerable, if unimaginative, Realtor refrain that transactions are not over until they *are* over.

Defaults by either seller or buyer do occur in my industry. In over thirty years of practice, I have personally been involved in only one, and fortunately it proved to be temporary. A pair of buyers of a listing of mine had endeavored to pull a fast one on my sellers, their relocation company, and me by pretending they'd never signed an addendum changing the sales price of the property in question from $800,000 to $850,000. Then they deliberately applied for a mortgage for 80 percent of the lower figure. Predictably, the lender's appraiser valued the property at $800,000. When I provided written proof that we did, indeed, have fully executed paperwork at a sales price of $850,000, the chiselers reluctantly tried to get the appraiser back to approve the higher number, but he refused to do so. The buyers did not materialize at the closing. I sat in the title company's assigned conference room, fifty minutes away from my office, for two hours to establish that my side, anyway, had been prepared to settle.

A week or so after their default, the buyers' attorney contacted me requesting a release of the buyers' down monies. Thank goodness that, like Hansel and Gretel with their bread crumbs, I keep meticulous records and had created a lengthy paper and email trail regarding the transaction. The lawyer cajoled, badgered, and finally threatened. Calmly I explained that I would welcome a lawsuit since my side was in the right and could easily prove it, which meant the judge would release the escrow monies to *my* clients, not his. I forget how we worked things out, loan-wise and appraisal-wise, but we did. After a month of attempted intimidation and shakedown, the buyers' pugilistic attorney advised his clients to come to the table and settle after all. Fifteen years later, the couple is still living in the house.

LAW #8: "It's not over until it's over."

Part Four

BEING ON TOP OF YOUR HOME PURCHASE

(BUYER)

Chapter 9

UNDERSTAND WHAT YOU SIGNED!

When an Agreement of Sale has been executed by *both* buyer and seller, the clock starts ticking. Deadlines for the former abound: for the two deposits, for inspections, for the mortgage application and mortgage commitment, for the settlement itself. Because missing a deadline exposes a purchaser to enormous risk, making sure one's clients don't miss any is a critical duty of a buyer's agent. Still, anyone in the process of acquiring ownership of the home he will soon consider his castle would be well-advised to keep careful track of these deadlines too.

The All-Important Home Inspection Contingency Deadlines

While I have never allowed any of my own buyers to miss a contractual deadline, I have seen other agents manage to do so. A common slip-up involves the Home Inspection Contingency provisions in my state's boilerplate Agreement of Sale. The contingency grants ten days for the buyer to inspect the property and present a formal Reply to

Inspections. It then allows five days for the seller and buyer to negotiate that Reply. The contingency allots a final two days for the buyer *proactively* either to execute with the seller a mutually acceptable Change of Terms Addendum or to terminate the transaction unilaterally in writing. Doing nothing is not advisable because the law deems the buyer who has "done nothing" in writing by the deadline to be buying the house—but here's the kicker: he's buying it "as is."

When my husband and I fell in love, I followed my own professional advice to "sell his house, sell her house, and purchase a new house." It so happened that the seventeen-day Home Inspection Contingency in the Agreement of Sale that Al. and his buyers had executed ended at midnight on Christmas Eve. While dining that night at an elegant local restaurant, I kept checking my email because it was inconceivable to me that my colleague Bobby would permit her clients to fall into the category of involuntarily buying Al.'s property "as is." Bobby did not get back to me until two days past the deadline! She wanted to know if Al. would accede to her buyers' full set of demands as expressed in their Reply to Inspections. No, I replied. Several days earlier I'd sent her the seller's written response to her buyers' demands, and that response had been Al.'s final and best offer. The buyers had not then executed with him a Change of Terms Addendum by the deadline. They had not unilaterally terminated the sales contract in writing either. In short, the buyers were now legally deemed to be buying "as is." Fortunately for them, Al. was still prepared to give them what he had originally offered—just not any more than that.

A similar case occurred a few years later. Sellers of mine accepted an offer on their home, the buyers submitted an aggressive Reply to Inspections, and the sellers responded in writing with the most they were willing to give. The deadline again passed with neither a Change of Terms Addendum getting executed by the parties nor the buyers submitting a written notice of termination. One can only imagine the buyers' wrath when their Realtor informed them that their side had blown an important deadline, making the subject of any seller credit moot. My clients had offered the couple $7,000. The upshot of this imbroglio was that the sellers proved willing still to give their buyers some money toward repairs out of the goodness of their hearts. It was not to the tune of $7,000, however.

Yet another case cropped up not long ago when a Home Inspection Contingency in an Agreement of Sale on a listing of mine happened to expire on Easter. The buyers' agent did not contact me until the day after Easter, unaware that her side no longer had any legal standing to negotiate seller credits and repairs. That was too bad for the buyers, since they had presented the longest laundry list of demands I had ever seen (two pages, single-spaced). In that case, I suggested my sellers choose several small, inexpensive repairs to do for the crushed buyers and leave it at that.

Incidentally, a buyer's Reply to Inspections should *never, ever* consist of a long laundry list of proposed seller credits and repairs. It is an immediate turnoff to the very person the buyer is endeavoring to persuade to help him out! An experienced buyer's agent will counsel her clients to prioritize the problems inspectors have discovered at the house and request the seller's help with only the most significant of them. When confronted with a long laundry list of what's wrong with his castle, the typical homeowner instantly takes umbrage and refuses to grant anywhere near as generous a credit as he would have if the buyer had tactfully zeroed in on just a few key problems. Once a buyer ticks off a seller, the game is up. The buyer can accept (by the deadline) what the ticked-off seller will give him, or he can terminate (again, by the deadline) the transaction in progress. Most buyers want the house, which is why playing their cards smartly during the home-inspection-related negotiations is so vital.

The All-Important Mortgage Commitment Deadline

Another pitfall for buyers and their agents is not taking the Mortgage Contingency's deadline for the mortgage commitment seriously. While missing the Home Inspection Contingency's final deadline can cost a would-be purchaser some money, missing the mortgage commitment deadline can cost him the actual house. You absolutely do not want to miss this potentially deal-breaking deadline if you are a buyer.

During our fifth real estate collaboration, a seller-friend of mine named Corinne accepted an offer on her house that, although not great, was good enough to allow her to move on with her life. The transaction progressed uneventfully until the buyer failed to produce a mortgage commitment by the deadline. Providentially for Corinne, an unsolicited backup offer had just materialized, and its proposed sales price, terms, and conditions were all superior to those in the offer my client had signed. The Mortgage Contingency of my state's standard Agreement of Sale contains a provision allowing the seller to kick the buyer out of a transaction *if the buyer misses the commitment deadline*. After grasping how she could benefit from her buyer's failure to provide a commitment on time, Corinne speedily availed herself of the unexpected but welcome opportunity to terminate her would-be sale to the first buyer and do business instead with the second.

Home Sale Contingency Pitfall for a Buyer

Home Sale Contingencies are used by those who do not financially qualify to purchase a new house without first selling their current one. If a homeowner can be persuaded to accept one as part of an Agreement of Sale, the contingency allows the buyer to "tag" the seller's house as his prospective new domicile while seeking a buyer for his own place. If he cannot find one within a mutually agreed-upon amount of time, the buyer is free to nullify the sales contract.

The risks a seller faces under the operation of a Home Sale Contingency are well recognized; they are responsible for the universal antipathy of homeowners to such a document. Less well recognized is the unique, potentially catastrophic problem the Home Sale Contingency poses for the buyer deploying it as part of a proposed sales contract. The problem arises from the *seller's* right, under such a contingency, to pull the plug on the transaction if presented with a superior second offer before the (first) buyer is in a financial position to waive the Home Sale Contingency.

I had a case in which for ten years, off and on, I discussed with an increasingly enfeebled husband and wife the desirability of selling their property and downsizing to a rental or retirement community. Finally, anxious family members prevailed on the couple to sell their beloved castle at last. Besides being dilapidated, the dwelling was chockablock full of books and papers, as befitted a professor emeritus trying to work on a major tome despite the gradual onset of Alzheimer's. By now the wife had full-blown Alzheimer's, macular degeneration, and major heart trouble that required around-the-clock nursing care at home. The pair was going broke. It was a terribly sad situation—and a race against time to get the couple out of the run-down, unkempt house and safely ensconced elsewhere.

The number of buyers that will purchase a house requiring extensive repairs and renovation is vastly smaller than the number that will step up to the plate for one in decent condition. It thus did not surprise me that buyers did not fall over themselves trying to see and bid on this one. Eventually, my sellers and I received an offer that included a Home Sale Contingency, which meant that the proposed transaction would be contingent on the sale and settlement of the buyers' current property. Listing agents do not much like contingent offers of this sort because, as I've said, they present special, albeit usually manageable, risks to their sellers. At the end of the day, though, an Agreement of Sale contingent on the sale and settlement of the buyer's current home is better than no Agreement of Sale at all, and in that spirit, I recommended my clients execute the offer.

When my fellow Realtor had given me the offer originally, I did not recognize the version of the Home Sale Contingency she was using. "Do you really want to use that particular form, Linda?" I had asked. "It doesn't have a normal kick-out clause that gives the buyer a short window in which to satisfy the contingency—if he can—and thereby remain in the deal. *Your* form permits the seller unilaterally to cancel the transaction with no warning at all." My colleague was unconcerned. "It's the only version of the Home Sale Contingency I could find in my office when I was preparing the papers, Joey."

At the time of this exchange, I had no premonition that something catastrophic would happen to Linda's buyers down the road. Frankly, it is doubtful whether a kick-out clause in their Home Sale Contingency would have protected them from losing the house under the specific circumstances in which they would later find themselves. However, a kick-out clause *would* have given them a day or two's clear warning of what the seller was about to do to them.

After executing the Agreement of Sale, my professor proved not entirely pleased by the contingent offer he and his wife had accepted. Repeatedly he now enjoined me to continue marketing and trying energetically to turn up a stronger offer. "If you can find a stronger offer," he insisted, "I will have no qualms about terminating the Agreement of Sale I am presently in." That his buyers would be totally blindsided in such a scenario did not bother him; it was Linda's form that allowed him to do so, after all. I could not fault my client; he and his spouse were running out of money.

Miraculously, a second set of buyers eventually popped up out of nowhere with an outstanding offer. It boasted a higher sales price and faster settlement than the offer my clients had already signed. Adding icing to the cake, the second offer was not weighed down with a Home Sale Contingency or even a Mortgage Contingency—the purchasers wanted to pay cash for the property! The professor was ecstatic. As the Realtor representing him, I was ecstatic too. I was also nervous because I try to be fair to all parties in a transaction, and I did not think it fair for Linda to imagine her buyers would wind up with my listing anymore, especially when, reportedly, they were just about to get their own property under contract. However, it would have been imprudent for me to allow my colleague to get wind of developments on my end, because I had not yet established that these new buyers were "for real" by verifying their financial bona fides.

The second set of buyers' financials desperately needed verifying because their story was outlandish: cash for the proposed transaction would be coming from Asia—from an account of a relative of one of the buyers. Before my sellers took the drastic step of terminating their sales contract with the first pair of buyers and accepting the new buyers' offer, I wanted to see that cash in the United States, safely deposited in the new buyers' local bank account. This took one week to accomplish. My sellers then summarily terminated our Agreement of Sale with the first party, as permitted by the version of the Home Sale Contingency the buyer's agent had injudiciously incorporated into the Agreement of Sale. They then signed an Agreement of Sale with the second party.

Like used car salesmen, Realtors are held in some suspicion by the public. Individual agents *can* be conniving and exploitative in dealing with sellers and buyers. But it also happens that sellers and buyers sometimes badly misapprehend the rules of the real estate game and cry foul where there has been none. Take the case just described, for example. An agent (yours truly) has acted within the law—in the best interests of her *clients* and at *their* behest. Everything she has done has been ethical and aboveboard. That does not mean individuals adversely affected by said agent's and her clients' actions will take the bad news sitting down.

Upon receiving my sellers' abrupt termination of the original Agreement of Sale, the disenfranchised buyers did not demand an explanation from their agent about the technical points in our contract that caused them to lose the property without warning or recourse. Instead, they stormed into my office and held me hostage for over an hour in one of our conference rooms. Angrily they challenged the legality of my clients' decision and violently berated me for presumably facilitating it. Much as I wanted calmly to explain the mechanics of a Home Sale Contingency to them, getting a word in edgewise proved impossible.

These purchasers were understandably distraught. Having their own home under contract at last, they now would have nowhere to go if my clients declined to sell to them. The couple insisted I phone the professor and ask him to reconsider his decision. I went back to my private office and made the call. Predictably, my client reiterated that he still wanted more money, a faster settlement date, and a cash deal. Since the first set of buyers could not provide any of those things, he would go with a set of buyers that could. The terms of the Agreement of Sale's Home Sale Contingency clearly allowed him to do so.

The upshot of this contretemps was that the first set of buyers filed a complaint against *me* with the state oversight authority. Although totally frivolous and quickly dismissed, the complaint shocked me. If the buyers had felt impelled to take anyone to task, it should have been their *own* Realtor.

LAW #9: "Time is of the essence."

LAW #10: "If a party to a transaction doesn't understand the sales contract and something bad happens, watch out—especially if you're the agent working with the party that *does* understand it."

Chapter 10

LEVERAGE YOUR AGENT'S EXPERTISE

I t is increasingly asserted that Realtors are practically obsolete, that residential properties can these days get bought and sold pretty much without professional intermediaries. True, we have the internet, which enables buyers to vet listings online for themselves and no longer rely on an agent to screen and select properties for them to see. Frankly, I miss the old days in the business for this reason: there is a unique professional satisfaction in gradually understanding a client's needs and wants, finding a new listing (or sniffing out a property soon coming to market) that would be perfect for that client, showing the client the place as soon as possible, and discovering one has hit the nail on the head! Because of the internet, though, buyers now tend to find their new home themselves instead of depending on a Realtor to find it for them. Of my last eleven sales as a buyer's agent, eight sets of clients were local and bought a property they had originally identified from internet research. The three sets of clients that relied on me to find their new home were out-of-state luxury buyers relocating for professional reasons.

Despite the internet's streamlining of her responsibilities, a buyer's agent still has plenty to do to earn her keep—that is, to be of vital service to those in her professional care. Just because a buyer can house-hunt on the internet does not mean he is automatically savvy enough to make a shrewd purchase of a new residence without professional assistance. Remember, we are talking about the most expensive acquisition of most people's lives. We are talking about grave downside risk for buyers with no experienced guide to alert them to potential dangers and keep them safely out of harm's way. That is why I earlier intimated that a buyer's agent is something of a magician: after months or years of giving client tutorials (usually in her own car), she manages to transform an uninformed home browser into an exquisitely prepared—and confident—home buyer ready to buy. Aside from a butterfly emerging from its chrysalis, is there anything more beautiful than this?

Ask Your Agent for Top-Notch House Sleuths

A crucial buyer decision is who to hire for the several home-related inspections. It is not only Realtors who are not created equal; it is also general inspectors, masons, septic system experts, mold experts, basement waterproofing specialists, and other property "detectives." A superlative buyer's agent will have a stable of superlative property investigators. If she does not, it is potentially a very serious problem for *you*.

In over three decades of practice, I have never had buyers discover, post-settlement, an issue at their new home. *Never.* The reason is that while wearing my buyer's agent hat, I make it my business to uncover both big and small issues at a property *during* the home inspection period. If the best sleuths I have in my professional orbit can accomplish that, then my buyers have maximum flexibility; they are not yet irrevocably committed to buying this particular residence. They can negotiate appropriate credits to stay in the deal, or (if they cannot get them) unilaterally terminate the transaction.

Over the years, my professional experts have uncovered hundreds and hundreds of structurally unsound roofs and basements, compromised joists and headers and sill plates, cracked heat exchangers and back-drafting water heaters (carbon monoxide), damp crawl spaces, and dangerously outdated (and now uninsurable) "knob and tube" electrical systems—to name but a few of the problems that may exist at a property. They say knowledge is power. For a home buyer investigating the underlying condition of his soon-to-be castle and learning whether it's wise to proceed with the transaction, it surely is.

The most inspections I've ever counseled a set of buyers to perform is nine or ten. Nine or ten is admittedly a huge number, but sometimes it is justified, indeed imperative, to get to the bottom of an array of issues my team's detectives are unearthing at a particular residence during the inspection process. For one sprawling mid-century contemporary that had seriously deteriorated, for example, we needed to obtain critiques of the overall condition of the house, its compromised stucco building envelope, its leaking tile roof, its basement moisture and mold issues, and its older pool and tennis court, in addition to reports on the presence or absence of either pests or radon. The projected remediation costs, once I got all the quotes worked up by the members of my Business Family involved in this challenging sale, totaled $200,000. So that's the amount I negotiated for my buyers. The dramatic, 6,500-square-foot home is, even as I write, energetically being given the multifaceted face-lift it so richly deserves.

Listen When Your Agent Identifies a Devious Seller

Sellers do not always react well to the findings of a prospective purchaser's inspectors. This was driven home to me when a colleague reported that her clients were balking at giving a credit to my buyers for structural repairs to the front exterior wall of their house. Years earlier, a previous homeowner had chopped a big hole in that solid stone facade, which was load-bearing, to accommodate a huge bay of windows. Although an impressive architectural feature, that row of windows was now visibly lopsided. According to my buyers' home inspector, the earlier owner had failed to do any compaction grouting to ensure the wall's continued structural integrity. As a result, the cracking foundation below was slowly subsiding. The buyers and I consulted a structural engineer, who informed us that the work needed at the front wall would cost between $10,000 and $15,000.

To establish that my team's expert was wrong about the front wall—that it, in fact, possessed no structural deficiencies whatsoever—the sellers' agent now produced what were billed as two "engineering reports" dating from 2005. Based on these ostensibly authoritative documents, the house had managed to sell in that year and again in 2011—*to the present owners*. My buyers and I were asked to review and take comfort in this paperwork too.

But the so-called engineering reports were highly suspicious. In the first place, they were not reports but merely letters. Second, neither letter had been penned by a structural engineer! The first was written in 2005 by an earlier *owner* of the property, a person who had purchased the house in 1995 and discovered the lopsided windows only after settlement. Now (2005) he wanted to sell the house—and preemptively make those windows a nonissue. To that end, he had composed a note for prospective purchasers explaining that he had long ago done a repair that stabilized the front wall's descent into the earth. His repair "guaranteed" that there could be no additional movement. Only a structural engineer, of course, is qualified to determine whether a repair to a structurally unstable wall has, in fact, stabilized it. The homeowner was not that. He was simply a seller hoping to unload his house without too much fuss over the subsiding front wall.

Despite the 2005 seller's reassuring letter, the eventual buyers for the property at that time had entertained reservations about the man's claim concerning the integrity of his house's front wall. To assuage their concern, the seller immediately volunteered to bring in an expert to examine it for them. Why the buyers would agree to this self-interested arrangement rather than investigate the wall with an expert of their own (or their Realtor's) choosing is unclear. The resultant second "engineering" report that was only a letter appears to have been a deliberate attempt at misrepresentation. Someone, not a structural engineer but writing on the *letterhead* of a big-time structural engineering firm, states that he did a "visual assessment of the cracks" and found nothing amiss.

I fight for my clients. The 2005 buyers had somehow wound up believing the then-seller's two self-serving "engineering reports." In time they sold the property to another pair of credulous buyers: the present sellers! After I explained to my clients what was suspect about the letters, they were not prepared to accept them uncritically: they still wanted a seller credit toward the job of fixing the wall. The sellers refused, and, predictably, the deal fell apart. My clients profusely thanked me for energetically looking out for their interests despite this unfortunate outcome. You cannot do business with everyone, they said.

You especially cannot do business with owners that refuse to acknowledge the actual scientific status of the bricks and mortar of their own abode.

Ask Your Agent to Evaluate Price Tags with You

Another area in which Realtors will forever be of great assistance to buyers involves helping them distinguish between listings priced right on the money, listings priced somewhat too high, and listings priced egregiously high. Presuming there exists a rule of thumb about price tags, clients new to house-hunting often ask how much to discount a listing's asking price to arrive at its fair market value. Most are guessing it is 10 percent. They are surprised when I explain that every single listing has to be evaluated on its own merits because sellers differ vastly in their ability to intuit the fair market value of their home to strangers (the buying public) as opposed to themselves.

Listing agents also differ vastly in their preferred pricing strategies and, more to the point, their own expertise at discerning the underlying value of specific properties at varying points in a real estate market cycle. Even when agents are spot-on with their pricing analyses, some will prove either too circumspect or too cynical to speak truth to power (their prospective clients). It is a simple matter for an agent deliberately to overprice a listing, get pats on the back from her sellers, and move the price tag downward from there when the property fails to sell. It is not so simple a matter for an agent to master the art of accurately predicting the range where properties *will* sell, forthrightly sharing her analysis with the homeowners, and making the case for strategically pricing the property.

Rely on Your Agent to Win a Bidding War

When a bidding war is in the offing, the buyer's agent who knows how to ensure her clients will win it is worth her weight in gold. This requires an accurate grasp of how well priced a particular property is, an ability to predict how other buyers will bid, and the talent for recommending to her buyers a top offer that will beat the highest competitor by a small amount. I invented my system during the 2002-2008 housing bubble as bidding wars became increasingly common in my market area. It consists of a matrix of bids and probabilities into which my clients plug how much they covet a particular house. I will say, "If you want to be 99 percent sure you'll land the property—you'll die if you don't get it—bid X. If you want 95 percent certainty, bid Y. If you are okay with an 80 percent chance of getting the house, bid Z."

The system worked like a charm for the duration of the craziness. Now that intense bidding wars are finally back after the extended market slump that followed the bubble, it is still working like a charm. In those instances where my buyers lose a property because they do not care to offer my 99 percent number, I always check later, once the sales price is public knowledge, to see whether my top number *would* have taken it. It always would have—by a narrow margin. That is the goal!

For a bidder who is going to need a mortgage to help finance his purchase, simply having the highest offer will not necessarily guarantee success. The reason is that the property will need to *appraise* for that high offering price for the purchaser to obtain his desired loan amount. A listing agent worth her salt would never want to expose her seller to that risk if she had an alternative to doing so.

A savvy *buyer's* agent will recommend that her clients write into the proposed sales contract that the property need only appraise for its *asking* price. From the perspective of a savvy *seller's* agent, that is a much safer bet than requiring it to appraise for a higher number than the appraiser might find justified using the existing "comps." This past summer, buyer-clients of mine declined to follow this simple but wonderfully effective strategy, thereby losing a ten-way bidding war to a (lower-paying) cash purchaser. Learning their lesson, they followed my advice with their next offer on a property—and promptly won a four-way bidding war. Adding icing to the cake, the property wound up appraising for its sales price, which meant my buyers did not need to put any additional cash into the deal.

One last tip regarding winning a bidding war is this: if it looks like there will be multiple bids, a smart buyer's agent will recommend that her clients bring a home inspector along on their showing appointment. If the prospective buyers do not care for the house, it is squandered pocket change and a small mistake. If they love the place, though, and their inspector confirms that the house is in good underlying shape, the buyers may feel confident in submitting an offer with *no* Home

Inspection Contingency. By following this strategy, the buyers of an enterprising colleague of mine recently won a vigorous bidding war on an immaculate new luxury listing of mine.

Ask for Enlightenment about Risks

I have shared stories about colleagues who did not keep their buyer-clients safe from harm—either by making sure they met their transaction deadlines or by addressing the inherent peril of a Home Sale Contingency by introducing mitigating language into the sales contract. There are many, many other things as well that can trip up a buyer. Inquire what they are so *you* do not inadvertently receive a nasty surprise.

Case in Point: On-site Septic System Risk

A colleague of mine represented buyers who had just put under contract a mansion on seven acres that I represented. In casual conversation, my seller now chanced to mention that he pumped out the on-site septic system three times a year. I was in shock: *three* times? Immediately I insisted he amend his formal Seller's Disclosure statement to include that fact. He resisted. I insisted. Once I had his dated initials on the change in the revised document, I quickly gave it to the buyer's agent, requesting that she have her clients also initial and date the change. She good-naturedly obliged, not grasping the dire implications of pumping out a septic system several times a year instead of just once (at most). During the general home inspection and on-site septic inspection, the buyer's agent did not bring the frequency of the pumping to the inspectors' attention. The system was deemed to be in good working order, the property went to settlement, and that was that.

Well, not entirely. The following year, my colleague phoned me in a panic. The on-site septic at the seven-acre estate had failed, and her buyers were about to sue the seller, our mutual brokerage company, and us agents. "Cathie," I soothed, "on what earthly basis could they sue? As soon as I learned how often my client was pumping out that darn system, I prevailed on him to note it on the Seller's Disclosure, and at my behest you had your buyers initial that extra dollop of information. There was no misrepresentation. They won't sue."

They did not sue. Of course, a sharper buyer's agent would have understood the risk of imminent failure of any septic system that was being pumped out frequently and would have taken pains to see that it was investigated thoroughly by a top-notch expert. If that expert had established that the system wasn't long for this world, the buyers could then justifiably have requested a seller credit of $30,000–$35,000 for a new system. Instead, in this case, they were caught unawares with a failed system in their first year of ownership and had to pay for a new one themselves.

Case in Point: Risk of Living in a Flood Zone

Increasingly risky to buyers is purchasing a property in an officially designated flood zone. For those financing their home purchase, obtaining flood insurance will be mandatory. Private insurers now exist, but historically insurance has been handled by FEMA's National Flood Insurance Program (NFIP). Understanding it requires a familiarity with the arcana of Elevation Certificates, the various rating categories, the rating appeals process, and the local impact of the latest FEMA revision of the nation's flood maps (now increasingly frequent in response to climate change). A Realtor who is familiar with these things is a rare bird—and a valuable asset to her clients. Right now, I have buyers under contract to purchase a house deemed just last year to require flood insurance (there is a creek running along the edge of the property). Besides helping these clients understand and acquire flood insurance (they opted to go through a private vendor), I have made a point of underscoring what could otherwise prove a nasty surprise down the road—that while their mortgage rate is fixed for the life of the loan, their flood insurance rate is susceptible to rising over time.

Use Your Agent for Help Long-Term

Following my strategy of making sure I was paying close attention post-settlement to former buyers, I chanced one day to check in with Shireen six or seven years after she and her husband had closed on their new home. To my horror, I learned that they had recently developed a swamp in their backyard. "It's so bad, Joey," my friend confided, "I can't let either the children or the dogs go outside; it's too muddy." Upon learning Shireen had gotten a $75,000 remediation proposal from a civil engineer, I flew into action. "I don't think it's a civil engineer you need to solve water problems in your yard; it's an exterior water management expert. I already have Jeff, the best there is, in my Business Family. Why don't I corral him for us? We can meet you at your house to review the plan you have and see what Jeff would do differently, if anything." Shireen gratefully acceded.

I knew Jeff was amazing because he had saved my own property from becoming unsalable owing to a sudden swamp that developed in my side and front yards after twenty-six years of owning a home on very dry land. As soon as my erstwhile client unfurled the civil engineer's remedial plan on her kitchen table for Jeff and me to review, even I could see that the proposed repairs were totally off base: they would not begin to solve the drainage issues in the yard, not to mention ominous water problems now developing inside the home as well. Jeff devised a marvelously appropriate plan in its place, and since implementation, the yard has been bone-dry. While he was at it, Jeff solved the water drainage issue in the next-door neighbor's yard too.

By staying in touch with a vast constituency of former clients, I can perform small miracles from time to time. Several years ago, a couple

I reincorporated into my social circle after launching my guardian-Realtor-for-life campaign had a delicate problem. The husband, an attorney, was out of work. Worse, despite diligent efforts to find a new position in mid-life, Brian was not making much progress. Impressed by his good spirits in the face of adversity, I introduced him to multiple contacts of mine that might prove helpful. Nothing worked out. Then, one Sunday night months later, I received a phone call from an acquaintance I liked very much. It seemed she was on the board of a certain charity dear to her heart, and Brian was one of the applicants for the job of running it. She had looked up his friends on Facebook and knew two of them: another person and me. What could I tell her about Brian's character and temperament? I gave an enthusiastic ten-minute speech—I pretty much knew the guy inside and out by this time even though our real estate transactions had occurred in the distant past—and, to my erstwhile client's relief, he won the post of executive director.

Choose a Compatible Agent

Emotional compatibility is important in buyer-Realtor partnerships. You do not want, for example, to work with someone who is not data-oriented if you are; it's a prescription for terminal mutual frustration. All ambitious agents naturally wish to broaden their potential client pool by enlarging the number of personality types for whom they are a decent fit. Still, at the end of the day, a particular Realtor will not be a great match for *everyone*.

In 2008, for instance, as one of my young Himalayan cats lay critically ill in a suburban animal hospital, a wishy-washy buyer of mine changed her mind for the last time on my watch. This woman had initially been looking at properties in both the exurbs and the suburbs—a wide swath of territory. After numerous showings in both areas, Molly announced that she had now definitely ruled out all remote locations. Nonetheless, that night when Cabrillo was near the point of death, she insisted I show her yet another listing in the exurbs. I did it, returned to the vet, put the terminally sick feline down, and fired the woman. Other agents may be able to tolerate persistently inconsistent clients, but I find I just cannot.

In the best collaborations, buyers love their Realtor and their Realtor loves them. "You went so far beyond the call of duty on our behalf that I will be eternally grateful," wrote one satisfied client of mine. That client, a prominent academic, originally had teamed up with an agent of an incompatible stripe. Someone had recommended he try me since I seemed to mesh with university types. At the end of our collaboration, the professor paid me the compliment of saying that, on top of my helping his family find a forever home, "I think we have actually become friends." In my book, there is no higher praise than that.

**LAW #11: "Never commoditize Realtors:
there are the great, the good, the middling,
the incompetent, and the disastrous."**

Part Five

APPROACHING SAFE HARBOR

Chapter 11

MONKEY WRENCHES

Sometimes no significant roadblocks appear on a Realtor's way to closing deals and proceeding worry-free to settlement. Sometimes small or medium-size hurdles crop up. Other times, though, all hell breaks loose.

Lawyerly Meddling

One category of monkey wrench arises from the circumstance that most real estate agents have not gone to law school. Despite that deficit in our education, we handle legal documents constantly in our work, preparing listing contracts, Buyer's Agency Contracts, and Agreements of Sale as well as addenda thereto and terminations thereof, to mention just the most common. Without formal legal training, we use boiler-plate forms drawn up by the federal government, the state's Association of Realtors, and our own brokerage companies. Inventing legal language ourselves and deploying it in contracts is strongly discouraged for the simple reason that it might prove to carry legal implications beyond what we intended and could land the company—and us—in a lawsuit.

While Realtors know not to muck around with real estate documents, most especially the all-important sales contract itself, no one seems to have told attorneys not to muck around with them either. This has caused many a problem and tanked many an otherwise viable transaction. One recent case of mine involved a seller who wanted to have his attorney look over the final version of a proposed Agreement of Sale before signing. The attorney wanted one change—that the paperwork specify that the purchasers, rather than the seller, would pay for any survey their title company might require.

Neither the selling agent nor I, the listing agent, had any idea what in our standard sales contract the attorney could possibly be responding to in making such a weird stipulation. Nonetheless, the buyers' Realtor ran it by his clients, who refused to agree without even being told what the specific referent in the Agreement of Sale was. "Page 8, Paragraph 16(c)," my seller informed me.

Live and learn! There indeed *is* verbiage in our sales contract about title companies, surveys, and sellers paying for said surveys in the event a title company ever calls for one. Even after being made aware of this arcane provision in the Agreement of Sale, however, the buyers were put off by the seller's picayune demand that the boilerplate language be altered in his favor. As the night wore on with no resolution to the impasse, I realized the transaction would soon be in jeopardy. It was clearly time to help my client, an esteemed university dean, put things in perspective.

I have found that emails are more effective than conversations in delicate impasses because they do not require the other party instantly to become defensive and dig in his heels. Rather than reflexively contest my position, that other party is afforded an opportunity to let its implications sink in. "While appreciating your attorney's point," I thus wrote my seller, "I personally have never in all these years seen a title company request such a thing. Of course, for forty years the Titanic's

Captain Smith had never encountered an iceberg before either. The cost to you on the off chance the buyers' title company demands a survey is less than $3,000. We are selling a $1,000,000 property, preferably tonight, while we still have the buyers' attention. Please decide how you'd like to proceed." My seller signed posthaste.

One of my would-be transactions that never got off the ground owing to attorney interference involved an outstandingly successful businessman whose first career had been as an outstandingly successful lawyer. The gentleman requested my help in selling his current residence and finding and purchasing a new one for him and his fiancée. In due course, we identified a promising candidate for the couple's new home, and I prepared an offer. Before signing it, David—against my advice—marked up the entire sales contract from beginning to end as only an honest-to-god lawyer knows how to do. Now only another attorney could possibly grasp the legal implications of his deleting entire paragraphs and making interpolations both short and long on every single page of my state's boilerplate Agreement of Sale! Although my client surely believed he was protecting himself every which way, what he achieved with his marked-up contract was to "protect" himself right out of owning the house.

The providential sequel to this story is that when, a year and a half later, we finally found another alluring property on which to bid, David offered the full asking price of $1,950,000 the first day it was listed and introduced not a single alteration into the sales contract. Sometimes in real estate, as in actual life, you are better off trusting the odds, taking a leap of faith that things will work out, than electing to pit yourself against your fellow man, demanding one or more protections before you'll take a single step toward your own overriding goal. In my one client's case, that goal was speedily unloading a vacant luxury property for which he no longer had any use whatsoever. In my other client's case, the goal was acquiring a beautiful residence for his new life with a cherished new spouse.

An Imploding Loan Officer

Except for my personal assistant, virtually no one is a more essential part of my real estate practice that my mortgage expert. I am very fussy about whom I select to work with because verifying buyers' financial capacity and making sure those who require mortgages secure them are nitty-gritty components of any Realtor's business. Typically, my anointed specialist is with me for years.

Perhaps because that is my style, I did not recognize the warning signs in one of the several individuals with whom I have aligned myself over the decades. First, little financing snafus started to occur. Then larger problems began to mar the smooth progression of my transactions from start to finish. One egregious error occurred when my financial specialist failed to perform the all-important task of verifying up-front the financial bona fides of a new set of buyers of mine. Only after we had put an attractive assemblage of bricks and mortar under contract did one of the buyers express concern about getting needed funds from relatives in China in a timely manner. Shocked by this crucial admission (it *can* be hard to get money out of China), I was compelled to abort the transaction and profusely apologize to the listing agent for having inadvertently placed both of us in a position where this would become necessary.

This loan officer had violated my trust by not performing her sacred duty of ascertaining these new buyers' financial strength *before* I even put them into my car, much less started submitting offers on their behalf. You might ask why I did not drop her right then and there. In retrospect, I should have. However, top-drawer mortgage experts are not easy to come by. At the time, it struck me as acceptable to soldier on, believing that my partner's odd ethical lapse was an aberration, not a harbinger of a tragic "new normal." As finance-related issues proliferated and worsened over the next several years, I was at a complete loss to account for them. How could a professional with a proven track record for excellence gradually devolve into a caricature of herself?

Matters came to a head when my loan expert did not materialize for a particular settlement. The closing officer urgently required her presence due to gross errors he had uncovered in her calculations of the final figures. Several times I called her cell phone from the settlement table, asking where she was. "On the road, on the way," she repeatedly informed me. Over two hours later, when the closing officer had fixed all the numbers and gotten everything straightened out by himself, we concluded the settlement and adjourned. My loan expert had never arrived.

The good news is that a jeopardized settlement got salvaged by the quick thinking of a smart closing officer and the cooperation of my annoyed buyers, who were forced to make a second trip to their bank since the absent loan expert had significantly underestimated how big a cashier's check they needed to obtain. The bad news is that, over a handful of years, a formerly stellar mortgage consultant mentally deteriorated before my eyes. Since my mother had developed early-onset Alzheimer's in her fifties, I knew that what I was witnessing with my financial expert was not that. But what could it be? I'll never know. Whatever the cause, I was sorry to see my very capable old friend disappear.

Underwater Sellers

Another type of monkey wrench that occasionally gets thrown into the mix arises when a seller is underwater—that is, owes more on his property than what he can fetch for it in the marketplace. I have been involved in two such transactions this year. The first one was relatively simple since the lender was a private party, a wealthy friend of the sellers, and prepared to forgive $300,000 worth of the sellers' debt to him so that our sale could proceed. The second transaction, which is ongoing, is anything but simple because the lender is a bank. I have limited experience with foreclosures, deeds in lieu of foreclosure, and short sales. However, I have gleaned that banks dislike taking losses on their loans (this one is for roughly $1,180,000) and hence will procrastinate as long as possible before doing so. Early on, my buyers and I were given to understand that the bank would ultimately approve a sales price of $900,000, and we originally submitted an offer in that amount. However, now that my buyers' several inspectors have sleuthed out $100,000 worth of urgently needed repairs, we do not know whether the bank will be receptive to selling the property to us for $800,000. There is no telling how long we will have to wait to find out.

Revelations at Presettlement Walk-Throughs

Last-minute changes in a house's physical condition constitute a unique type of monkey wrench. Accompanied by their own agent and sometimes the seller's agent as well, buyers routinely do a walk-through of their home-to-be just prior to closing. Its purpose is to confirm that the residence is in the same shape as it was at the time of their home inspections. If it is not, the purchasers have one last opportunity—at the settlement table itself—to negotiate an appropriate modification of the parties' sales contract.

(a) Gaining Access to the House

Finding an unpleasant surprise *at* a presettlement walk-through presupposes that a buyer's agent and her client(s) have had the opportunity to conduct one. One time, though, my clients and I could not gain access to a luxury home on which we were about to settle. The sellers had moved out two days earlier and left at the front door a key in a lockbox provided by their Realtor. No one had checked to see whether the key worked.

My team discovered it did not work. From their new condo across town, the sellers insisted that the key did work. The listing agent, who strangely decided to believe them rather than the buyers and me, declined to call a locksmith for us (we needed to get to the settlement on time!). The buyers made a video, which I forwarded to my colleague to demonstrate that the key did not even begin to fit the lock. Still no action.

Eventually, the listing agent told me that the wife-seller was climbing in her car and coming over to prove the key worked. By this point, I had long since sent my buyers on ahead to the settlement table to execute the necessary paperwork. They could safely do that because the closing officer had kindly offered not to finalize the transaction until we could conduct a satisfactory *post*-settlement walk-through.

I had been cooling my heels unproductively in the driveway for nearly three *hours* when a swooshing sound alerted me that a vehicle was pulling up beside mine. A woman emerged, marched purposefully up to the front door (I followed), easily unlocked it, and declared "there!" as she then spun around to face me. I was incredulous. "But, Marsha, you have just unlocked this house from a key on your own key chain, not the key from the lockbox. You are supposed to surrender all keys to the buyers at the time of settlement. Please take that key off your key chain and give it to me."

So reluctant had the sellers been to hand over the key to their beloved castle that they had made a (flawed) new copy of the key and left *that* for the buyers and me. They were evidently planning to keep the original.

(b) Missing "Fixtures" and/or "Inclusions"

Once inside a house, I have made any number of last-minute disagreeable discoveries. One set of sellers had removed all the fancy kitchen hardware, shown in advertising photos on the internet, and replaced it with Home Depot-quality hinges and pulls. This caused a row because, legally, such hardware falls into the category of "fixture" and is supposed to transfer with the property.

Another time when my buyers and I went for our presettlement walk-through, we discovered to our mutual consternation that the mansion's magnificent drapes had up and disappeared. They were supposed to have stayed put because the parties' fully executed Agreement of Sale had explicitly listed them as "inclusions." Anything listed as such in a sales contract is to remain in the house and transfer along with it to the buyer(s). We soon learned that the missing drapes were on a moving van en route to the sellers' new home. I asked for them to be returned and reinstalled immediately, after which I said my team would go to settlement. At that point, a major contretemps ensued.

It is important for a *buyer's* agent to insist that sellers act on any legitimate request *before* the house in question settles; it's the last time she will have any leverage. Once a property closes, the pressure is off the former owners. At that point, no one can reliably predict whether they will act on any verbal promise made before or at closing. They might—but, then again, they might not. These are not good odds for getting fancy drapes returned and professionally rehung by the previous owners at *their* expense.

I was dealing in this transaction with a Realtor known for her huge sales volume. She was also known for her temper. "Negotiating" with her proved disagreeable in the extreme. Still, if your job is to protect your clients from getting pummeled by a bully, there's nothing for it but to stand your ground, politely but firmly, and insist that you won't settle until the drapes are returned and reinstalled. Soon enough, the moving van materialized in the mansion's front courtyard. The tumult over the missing "inclusions" delayed the closing two or so hours.

(c) Collapsed Ceilings, Broken Locks, Floor Stains

Another time when I walked through a house with buyers just before settlement, we found the ceiling of one of the children's bedrooms collapsed and lying on the floor, a dusty heap of rubble. It turned out that the sellers' insurance would cover the cost of the necessary repair work, which was fabulous. Still, it took time to hammer out at the settlement table a protocol for how the job would proceed post-settlement and to codify the arrangements in a document both parties were amenable to signing.

In cases where a seller and a buyer cannot agree on an appropriate remedy to a problem only revealed during the walk-through, closings can last hours. I once sat for most of the day at a settlement table—the listing agent went home for five hours in the middle of it—waiting for an intransigent seller to accede to my buyers' request for a modest credit to pay for a new front-door lock (we'd discovered that the current one didn't work). Another time a seller of mine dying from melanoma stubbornly held up the settlement proceedings for so many hours that everyone—title company, seller, buyers, agents—was held hostage at the closing table into the night. The brouhaha arose from the buyers' belated discovery of a large hardwood floor stain that prior to their walk-through had been hidden under a large carpet.

(d) Water

Water can present a particular challenge at presettlement walk-throughs. I have seen basements flooded by burst water heaters, by garden hoses negligently left on near an exterior wall, and by ruptured pipes. Only once, though, have I witnessed an entire house flooded.

The Completely Flooded House

The property in question had a poignant backstory. Twelve years earlier, I had been referred to a man moving across the country to work at one of my area's many fine colleges. During our house search, he'd fallen in love with and purchased a sensationalistic contemporary featuring an indoor pool and adjacent recreation area of the sort attractive to single men who enjoy partying (a previous owner had been a professional football player). The residence was situated on a busy street and sat down toward the bottom of sloping terrain adjacent to a creek. Directly in front of the side-set dwelling loomed a very steep, eroding hillside with who knew what perched way up on its crest. My bachelor client loved the place despite the poor quality of its construction, which was noted in the general inspection report.

Over the years, Liam and I stayed in touch. At lunch one day he startled me by announcing that he would be moving again. I didn't like the news—Liam was a great guy. The prospect of collaborating to sell the splendorous contemporary would be welcome, however. I reached out the next week to follow up, but my friend was nowhere to be found—nowhere that I thought to look, that is.

It turned out that, two or three days after we'd dined together, Liam had been rushed to the hospital suffering from an intestinal blockage. Cancer was the eventual diagnosis. Grueling rounds of chemotherapy followed. Despite a couple of remissions that allowed my client to resume flying his plane and sailing his yacht, in the end he died.

Although the man himself was now gone, the vacant contemporary with the indoor pool and splashy game area remained. Since Realtors, like nature, abhor a vacuum, I was pleased to be asked to sell the property for the estate. The house was in poor condition, and I priced it accordingly. Considering it a diamond in the rough, young buyers of an associate of mine quickly put the new listing under contract. Everything went fine until the walk-through on the day of settlement.

The day *before* settlement my Business Family's deep-cleaning specialist had scoured the home's interior from top to bottom to make it squeaky clean for our young buyers. The day *of* settlement I met the excited purchasers and their agent at the property for the walk-through. We all greeted one another warmly and casually entered the house together. A horrific sight greeted us: mud and water were everywhere! During the heavy deluge in the middle of the previous night, part of that very steep slope the residence faced must have collapsed and catapulted acres of drenched hillside straight at—and into—the building. Fortunately, I think well on my feet when desperate. In a flash, I came up with a strategy to convince the young buyers and their agent (as well as the estate I represented) to close the sale, mud and water and incipient mold notwithstanding.

Initially, the shocked purchasers completely misunderstood where I was headed when I congratulated them on having this catastrophe strike before settlement and come to their attention literally on the way to it. The furious wife, who proved to be an attorney, demanded to know how I could trivialize an experience as devastating for them as viewing expanses of sludge in what was to have been their dream home. I explained that what I wanted to underscore for their benefit was the serendipity of discovering the mega-mess *now.* Had it occurred the next week—or even simply an hour after closing—they as the home's new owners would have been placed in an even more difficult situation than the one in which they currently found themselves.

Since, I continued, the hillside had collapsed on the estate's watch, not theirs, might it behoove the young buyers to mull over what in their view would constitute adequate compensation for completing the transaction on schedule? Under the ostensible reasonableness of this approach, the wife's ire gradually dissipated. After they retreated to one of the few dry corners of the house to confer privately, all I could catch were the unpromising words "newborn" and "mold."

Happily, a monetary adjustment came to the rescue, as it does so many times in ticklish real estate situations. In view of all the visible damage and best guesses as to remediation costs, my team wound up selling the soggy property for a great deal less than we had anticipated. On the other hand, we did sell it—and right on schedule to boot.

LAW #12: "Engage a Realtor with superior skills, because up to and including the settlement at which a property's legal transfer of ownership occurs, bizarre problems can surface."

EPILOGUE

GRATITUDE

To act as a true seller or buyer advocate, subsuming one's own interests under those of a client, is not for everyone. Some of my colleagues, frankly, cannot or will not do it. For me, however, unreservedly championing clients and protecting them from harm has proven gloriously fulfilling, most especially when said clients are both eager and thankful for my assistance. There is, I've come to believe, a certain quiet nobility inherent in a real estate professional that devotes herself unconditionally to those who depend on her expertise for the realization of their real estate needs, objectives, and (yes) dreams.

I was reminded of this upon receiving a nice note from a rather prickly seller whose house, which she had owned for decades, I had recently shepherded safely through closing. Trouble had started right after the checks were cut and I was putting on my coat to leave the settlement venue. The buyer's agent suddenly blurted out that he and his client had had a misunderstanding. It seemed the heat had not been working properly during the pair's presettlement walk-through of my listing several hours earlier. Oddly, he had neglected either to call me from the house to report it or to broach the matter with me during the lengthy settlement we had just pleasantly concluded.

My impression was that the buyer was now belatedly insisting that her agent pressure me to have my seller do something about the allegedly nonfunctioning thermostat *she* (not my client) now legally owned. I naturally reported the matter later to the seller (she had not attended closing), whose comment was that it had been working the day before when she had spent several hours at the house cleaning. That intelligence I promptly passed on to the buyer's agent.

Several days later, I received an email from that same agent informing me that an HVAC company had just examined the boiler, found it hazardous, and shut it down as a safety measure. New equipment would cost $13,000. The distressed buyer, who had wanted to move in right away with her young grandson but now obviously could not, was asking my client to contribute toward the cost of a replacement boiler.

It is unheard of for a buyer to request credits from a seller once a property has legally transferred ownership. That's the whole point of transferring ownership: anything wrong at a property discovered before the settlement *is* the seller's problem, but after the settlement it's the *buyer's* (unless the seller deliberately concealed one or more material defects, in which case a lawsuit against the seller may be in the offing). How could my colleague brazenly come to me, days after our closing, and ask with a straight face for the seller to subsidize the buyer's purchase of a new boiler? The request was preposterous.

"I am at a loss to understand on what grounds you and your client believe the seller should rightly subsidize work done at the house post-settlement," I wrote Russ. Noting that the buyer had had a thorough general inspection of the residence conducted by an expert of her choosing, I reminded my colleague that many substantive findings were documented in that expert's inspection report. At its "boiler system" section, I said, quoting the inspector, "Rust and corrosion were noted." I underscored to Russ that the buyer's inspector had explicitly called for the *entire system* to be evaluated. Because he and his client chose to do that post-settlement rather than during the buyer's formal inspection period, I wrote that "I perceive no liability or responsibility on the seller's part."

I sent a copy of this email to my normally testy and fiercely headstrong seller and to her real estate attorney. My client quickly set me the nice note alluded to above. "Thank you for your response to Russ and for taking care of me." How can your heart not melt when a client expresses gratitude for being taken care of? Don't we all secretly want to receive first-class treatment from dedicated, non-conflicted advisors as we navigate through life's uncharted (to us) waters?

Mentioning the desirability, if rareness, of non-conflicted advisors reminds me to observe that many advisors—alas, in many fields (my husband deals with them in the world of trusts and estates)—are, in fact, conflicted. Take the buyer's Realtor mentioned above. In a shocking lack of professionalism, Russ did not actually attend *his own buyer's* general home inspection at my listing. His client might not have known that (she did not attend either), but it was an egregious ethical lapse nonetheless. That left only me, the conscientious listing agent, on the premises with the buyer's general inspector—and I learned a great deal about the property over the course of two hours.

Much more was suspect than the house's boiler. Most worrisome to me at the time were suspected structural issues with the garage walls. Besides calling for a review of the entire boiler system, accordingly, the inspector in his inspection report had called for a structural engineering examination of the garage. Why hadn't Russ called me for appointments to bring an HVAC expert and a structural engineer to the property during his buyer's allotted inspection period? He was either wholly incompetent or conflicted, preferring to prioritize making a sale over doing right by his client. Doing right by his client, in this case, would have entailed vigorously investigating potentially serious issues at the house while his buyer *still had a chance to negotiate credits or get out of the deal if she so chose.*

But consider this: what would have happened to Russ if his buyer *had* become aware of the house's issues and elected to get out of the deal while she still had a chance? To earn a commission, he would then have needed to slog around town with her for as many more months or years as it took to find another property she wanted to bid on. Perhaps he found it easier to skip the inspection, disregard the inspector's findings (assuming he read the report), leave his buyer in the dark about the implications of those findings, grab a quick commission, and fail to inform the new homeowner that, legally speaking, from the close of settlement onward (seller malfeasance excepted) all problems found at the house were now *her* responsibility.

❦

Out of the blue, I received a curious text from former clients: "We've got a new pool boy!!" The message initially flummoxed me because I had shared my own pool man, Dave, with the buyers in question once they had finally purchased a new home (on our fourth attempt), one accoutered with a pool. Then I saw the photo and the accompanying note. "Remember those babies, Joey? They've gotten big. We were so anxious about having a pool for the first two years, and now we are loving it!!!" Pictured was one of the twins, the little boy, just barely wielding a pool skimmer. My client ended with these touching words: *"Thank you for helping us find our forever house."*

That's what I do. I help people find and purchase their forever house … and then eventually I sell it when they discover forever does not last indefinitely.

THE TWELVE LAWS
OF REAL ESTATE

LAW #1: "Selling and buying real property is a *very* touchy business."

LAW #2: "Academics publish or perish; Realtors sell or perish."

LAW #3: "The seller may propose, but it is the *buyer* who disposes."

LAW #4: "At the beginning, in the middle, and at the end, it's always about price."

LAW #5: "To get paid what you're worth, insist on getting paid what you're worth."

LAW #6: "To stay out of legal trouble, learn the facts, and *disclose* them."

LAW #7: "The first offer is the best offer."

LAW #8: "It's not over until it's over."

LAW #9: "Time is of the essence."

LAW #10: "If a party to a transaction doesn't understand the sales contract and something bad happens, watch out—especially if you're the agent working with the party that *does* understand it."

LAW #11: "Never commoditize Realtors: there are the great, the good, the middling, the incompetent, and the disastrous."

LAW #12: "Engage a Realtor with superior skills, because up to and including the settlement at which a property's legal transfer of ownership occurs, bizarre problems can surface."

ACKNOWLEDGMENTS

To legions of appreciative clients over many years, I offer my heartfelt thanks for engaging my services, becoming my dear friends, and teaching me important lessons in how to live well during our fleeting time on Earth. In *Open House!* I have endeavored to share your collective wisdom, which I strongly believe deserves to be known to more than one fortunate long-practicing Realtor.

Several individuals have been instrumental in putting me in touch with Terri King, the chief marketing officer at Buffini & Company, whose exceptional founder and chairman has been an inspiration to me for many years. Terri, in turn, introduced me to the founder of Jane Wesman Public Relations Inc. Jane's expert guidance and wisdom proved invaluable. It was through her that I because acquainted with Kathy Meis, the founder and chief executive officer of Bublish. Kathy was extremely patient and supportive throughout the actual publication process.

Finally, I want to mention how touched I was that Frank May, Jr., my broker/manager, expressed interest in the manuscript before it had gone to press. With his cautionary advice, he saved me from pitfalls in which I would otherwise unwittingly have become ensnared. As for his reaction to the substance of my opening chapters, it ranged from extremely positive to "LOL!" This gives me hope that I have managed to execute my mission in an entertaining manner. That mission has been to shine a bright, discerning light on the normally opaque workings of an essential industry used by 66 percent of American adults at least once—and often (thankfully) much more than that.

INDEX

GLOSSARY

AGENT, REAL ESTATE

A licensed real estate salesperson in a particular state; colloquially used interchangeably with REALTOR (Realtor), which term denotes a member of the National Association of Realtors (NAR)

Buyer's agent (selling agent)

A real estate professional working with a buyer

Seller's agent (listing agent)

A real estate professional working with a seller

AGREEMENT OF SALE

A fully executed written contract according to which a buyer agrees to purchase real property and its owner agrees to sell it, according to concise yet carefully spelled out terms and conditions in that contract

Exclusions in

Items that would normally transfer with the house in a sale but which a seller and a buyer specify in the Agreement of Sale will *not* be included

Inclusions in

Items that would not normally be included in a home sale but which a seller and a buyer specify in the Agreement of Sale *will* be included

BUYER'S AGENCY CONTRACT

A brokerage company document in which a buyer pledges to be responsible for paying a specified commission if he purchases a home during the period of the contract

CLEAR TITLE

A title with no liens or other types of encumbrances of any kind

CLOSING (SETTLEMENT)

A real estate transfer of ownership's final stage, in which the property is legally conveyed from seller to buyer via deed, title, and keys to the house

COMPARABLE SALES (COMPS)

Recent sales in a neighborhood that appraisers and agents use to help them gauge fair market value for a "subject property"

DEFAULT

The name for cases in which a transaction does not settle because one of the parties does not show up at the closing

FEDERAL EMERGENCY MANAGEMENT AGENCY (FEMA)

The national agency, part of Homeland Security, that through mapping and re-mapping keeps up-to-date data on the country's high-risk flood zones and the degree of risk different zones pose for residential real estate located within their boundaries

FIXTURE

Any item identified in the Agreement of Sale as such and therefore required to transfer, along with the house, to a buyer at settlement

FLOOD INSURANCE
Protection against flood damage, advisable for cash owners living in a FEMA-designated flood zone and mandatory for any owner with a mortgage

FOR SALE BY OWNER (FSBO)
A homeowner that is selling his property with no help from a real estate agent

HOME INSPECTION CONTINGENCY (in AOS)
The section within the Agreement of Sale that governs the process by which a buyer conducts inspections on a property, negotiates their findings with the seller, and then either executes a mutually agreeable Change of Terms Addendum with the seller or unilaterally terminates the transaction in writing—by a specified deadline

HOME SALE CONTINGENCY (in AOS)
A document attached to an Agreement of Sale that makes the contemplated transaction contingent on the buyer's selling his own house

HOUSING BUBBLE
A temporary (but sometimes years-long) rapid run-up in home values that ends in collapse

MATERIAL DEFECT
A specific issue with a system or component of a home that may negatively impact its value or pose an unreasonable risk to people—and which a seller must disclose to buyers if he is aware of it

MORTGAGE CONTINGENCY (in AOS)
A section within the Agreement of Sale that spells out the rules and deadlines governing a buyer seeking financing as part of a real estate transaction

MORTGAGE COMMITMENT
Documentation showing a lender's approval of a buyer's mortgage application, due on a date specified in the Mortgage Contingency

NATIONAL FLOOD INSURANCE PROGRAM (NFIP)

A FEMA-sponsored flood insurance program available nationwide to all participating communities

PRESETTLEMENT WALK-THROUGH

A tour taken prior to settlement by the buyer(s), the buyer's agent, and sometimes the seller's agent to confirm that the residence is in the same condition as obtained at the time of the home inspections

REPLY TO INSPECTIONS

A form used by a buyer for negotiating purposes, post-inspections, to indicate to a seller what amount of money and/or repairs he considers it equitable for the seller to provide in view of the findings

RED FLAG

Anything inside a house or above, on, or in the ground associated with it that could alarm a buyer

SELLER'S DISCLOSURE

A lengthy, detailed legal document in which a seller testifies to the current condition of many different systems of his residence and answers questions about specific issues at or potentially affecting the property

TITLE REPORT

A document that describes the legal status of a property and conveys related information about the property's history—ownership transfers, mortgage records, the existence of any liens or other types of encumbrances, and so on

UNDERGROUND STORAGE TANK (UST)

Buried storage tank (e.g., oil, propane)

WHITE ELEPHANT
A residential property sufficiently unconventional that it repeatedly has difficulty selling and re-selling

WIRE FRAUD (in real estate)
Fraud involving the wire transfer of funds, in which the transferring funds for a real estate purchase are hijacked by an imposter

CPSIA information can be obtained
at www.ICGtesting.com
Printed in the USA
BVHW041101140521
607050BV00011B/1636